MARCO POLO

Insider Tips

PRAGUE

SWEDEN

DENMARK

Baltic Sea

LITHUANIA

NETHER-LANDS

Berlin

Warsaw

POLAND

GERMANY

Prague

Frankfurt

CZECH REPUBLIC

SLOVAKIA

Munich

HUNGARY

AUSTRIA

← INSIDE FRONT COVER:
THE BEST HIGHLIGHTS

The best Insider Tips → p. 4

INSIDER TIP

Best of ... → p. 6

Sightseeing → p. 26

Food & Drink → p. 64

4   THE BEST INSIDER TIPS

6   BEST OF ...
● GREAT PLACES FOR FREE p. 6
● ONLY IN PRAGUE p. 7
● AND IF IT RAINS? p. 8
● RELAX AND CHILL OUT p. 9

10   INTRODUCTION

16   WHAT'S HOT

18   IN A NUTSHELL

24   THE PERFECT DAY

26   SIGHTSEEING
CASTLE QUARTER/HRADČANY,
LESSER TOWN/MALÁ STRANA,
OLD TOWN/STARE MĚSTO & JOSEFOV,
NEW TOWN/NOVÉ MĚSTO, IN OTHER
QUARTERS, OUTSIDE THE CITY

64   FOOD & DRINK
DINING OUT IN PRAGUE – CHEFS HAVE
FOUND INSPIRATION FURTHER AFIELD

74   SHOPPING
BOOKS, BEERS AND COLOURFUL
KNICK-KNACKS – WHERE TO BUY YOUR
SOUVENIRS

SYMBOLS

INSIDER TIP   Insider Tip

★   Highlight

●●●●   Best of ...

∿   Scenic view

☺ Responsible travel: fair
trade principles and the
environment respected

(*) Telephone numbers that
are not toll-free

**PRICE CATEGORIES
HOTELS**

Expensive   over 3,300 Kč

Moderate   2,000–3,300 Kč

Budget   under 2,000 Kč

The prices are for two people
sharing a double room during
high season (April–June, September, October and New Year)

**PRICE CATEGORIES
RESTAURANTS**

Expensive   over 450 Kč

Moderate   250–450 Kč

Budget   under 250 Kč

Prices for a main course with
no drinks

On the cover: Escape the crowds on charles bridge p. 38 | Trendy bars in Žižkov p. 82

CONTENTS

ENTERTAINMENT 82
FROM PUB TO CLASSICAL MUSIC –
PRAGUE IS THE PLACE TO BE IF YOU
WANT A GOOD NIGHT OUT

WHERE TO STAY 92
MONASTERY, HOSPITAL, TOWER –
PRAGUE'S HOTELS MEET ALL NEEDS

WALKING TOURS 100

TRAVEL WITH KIDS 106

FESTIVALS & EVENTS 108

LINKS, BLOGS, APPS & MORE 110

TRAVEL TIPS 112

USEFUL PHRASES 120

STREET ATLAS 124

INDEX & CREDITS 142

DOS & DON'TS 144

Shopping → p. 74

Entertainment → p. 82

Where to stay → p. 92

Street atlas → p. 124

DID YOU KNOW?
Books & Films → p. 33
Sightseeing with a difference
→ p. 47
Slavia or Sparta? → p. 48
Keep fit › p. 57
Relax & Enjoy → p. 58
Local specialities → p. 70
Gourmet restaurants → p. 72
Luxury hotels → p. 96
Budgeting → p. 115
Weather in Prague → p. 118

MAPS IN THE GUIDEBOOK
(126 A1) Page numbers
and coordinates refer
to the street atlas and orien-
tation map of Prague on p.
134/135
(0) Site/address located off
the map. Coordinates are also
given for places that are not
marked on the street atlas.
Hradčany and metro map inside back cover

**INSIDE BACK COVER:
PULL-OUT MAP →**

PULL-OUT MAP [M]
([M] A–B 2–3) Refers to the
removable pull out map

The best MARCO POLO Insider Tips

Our top 15 Insider Tips

INSIDER TIP Slow food Czech style

Want some good old-fashioned Bohemian cuisine? Well, you can still find it at the Lokál – or rather, it's back. Great pub in retro 1960s style with embroidered drapes and simple wooden benches → **p. 73**

INSIDER TIP Fast food Czech style

After the Velvet Revolution hamburgers almost replaced *chlebíčky*, but fortunately those delicious mayonnaise-drenched morsels live on. Those on sale at the Paukert deli are particularly recommended. They know how to serve them here, but then they should do. This shop has been in business since 1916 → **p. 77**

INSIDER TIP Prague's modern art factory

Art and design in this former industrial building is funky and cutting edge – the DOX is Prague's largest gallery for contemporary art. Plus a café and design shop → **p. 61**

INSIDER TIP Jazz on a grand scale in a small museum

He wrote many of the popular songs from the inter-war years – Prague's smallest museum recalls the life and work of Jaroslav Ježek → **p. 46**

INSIDER TIP Shops, a ballroom, a cinema and a club

The Lucerna Arcade opened at the start of the 20th century when multi-function malls were a groundbreaking concept (photo above) → **p. 100**

INSIDER TIP Prague's cake capital

If you step inside Myšák, then you can't be calorie-averse – it's cream gâteau heaven in a retro setting → **p. 65**

INSIDER TIP Modernist villa

Plain and white on the outside, open plan and colourful on the inside – visitors are welcome at the Müllerova villa, but by appointment only (photo below) → **p. 18**

INSIDER TIP **An all-round view from the tower**
During the communist era agents used this vantage point to keep an eye on western embassies, now tourists click away on their cameras. There's a great view from the tower of St Nicholas Church → **p. 40**

INSIDER TIP **The Infant Jesus of Prague**
For centuries, the faithful have made pilgrimages to the Jezulátko, a 45-cm (18-inch) high wax figure in the Church of Mary the Victorious → **p. 39**

INSIDER TIP **Coffee and ceramics**
Resplendent after renovation, the Art Nouveau tiles in the Café Imperial deserve a closer look → **p. 66**

INSIDER TIP **An old New World**
The picturesque cottages in the New World district (Nový Svět) are only a stone's throw from the grand palaces that surround the castle → **p. 34**

INSIDER TIP **Museum of the Resistance**
A small, but poignant exhibition – in 1942 the assassins of Reinhard Heydrich used the Cathedral of Saints Cyril and Methodius as a hide-out, until it was raided by the SS → **p. 56**

INSIDER TIP **Simple but beautiful**
If you like wearing contemporary rings, necklaces and bracelets, then look out for those bearing the Belda brand name → **p. 81**

INSIDER TIP **Through thick and thin**
There's a clever combination of convex and concave mirrors on Petřín Hill – take your camera into the maze and create your own wacky holiday snaps → **p. 105**

INSIDER TIP **Modern stage**
The Divadlo Archa is a centre for contemporary stage art and international productions with excellent performances – sometimes in public places throughout the city → **p. 90**

BEST OF ...

GREAT PLACES FOR FREE
Discover new places and save money

FOR FREE

● *Changing of the Guard at the castle*
Fanfares, marching in lockstep, uniforms – the *Changing of the Guard* in Hradčany takes place every day on the dot at noon and it wonww-wwwwwt cost you a penny (photo) → p. 29

● *Beer garden with views of the Vltava*
On hot days it can be hard to find a space on the wooden benches under the chestnut trees in the beer garden at Letná Park – the same goes for the nearby meadow. Draught *pivo* (beer) is sold at a drinks stall for one euro per plastic beaker. A good atmosphere and a spectacular view over the Old Town come free of charge → p. 90

● *The Golden Lane*
A visit to Prague's famous little lane, where Franz Kafka once lived, is simply obligatory. If you want to avoid the crowds, then come after 4pm in winter or 6pm in summer. And of course there's no admission charge → p. 31

● *Modern architecture – the Dancing House*
Great art and it costs nothing. The *Dancing House* by top architect Frank O. Gehry and local architect Vlado Milunic is quite a spectacle; it has become a symbol for the new face of Prague → p. 58

● *A tour of Prague's film locations*
Where did 007 give his pursuers the slip in 'Casino Royale'? Where was Miloš Forman's Oscar-winning 'Amadeus' filmed? Where did Angelina Jolie once stand against the Prague skyline? Go to the tourist office and pick up the free city map entitled *Lights! Camera! Prague!* ... and no box office → p. 23

● *A visit to the national cemetery*
Smetana, Dvořák and a number of other Czech cultural heroes are buried at *Vyšehrad Cemetery*. Many of the 200 graves here are mini-works of art – a stroll among the tombstones is like a free museum tour → p. 59

●●●● Dots in guidebook refer to 'Best of ...' tips

ONLY IN PRAGUE
Unique experiences

● *The Jewish Quarter*
Time has stood still in this ancient part of Prague. Take a walk at night through the cobbled streets and, you never know, you could find the legendary golem lurking around the next corner → **p. 41**

● *A beer with the locals*
There are not many pubs and bars around the Old Town Square where the locals feel at ease. *U parlamentu* is different – there's always something going on here → **p. 73**

● *The market by the Havel church*
There has been a market in the shadow of the Havel church since the Middle Ages. In the past it was fruit and vegetables, now it's more likely to be jewellery and objets d'art. Even so, trade is usually brisk → **p. 80**

● *Jazz in the cellar*
The Czechs are said to be masters of improvisation and that also applies to music. Prague has had a reputation as a jazz town for several decades. If you want to hear the best of the local talent, then the *Agharta* cellar club is the place to go → **p. 88**

● *Franz Kafka and Prague*
Franz Kafka had a rather difficult relationship with his home town – and the Czechs did not warm to the celebrated author, who wrote in German. Discover more out about the man's troubled life in the *Franz Kafka Museum* → **p. 38**

● *A famous landmark*
Tourists, street musicians, traders – during the day the crowds converge on the *Charles Bridge* and sometimes you can hardly move. Nevertheless, the medieval structure continues to be a source of fascination. If you want to see the bridge at its best, be there either early in the morning or later on in the afternoon (photo) → **p. 47**

● *Fierce fights on ice*
The sport that can move Praguers to a state of euphoria or plunge them into deep gloom is *ice hockey*. Tensions rise around the city when the two teams from the capital, Slavia and Sparta, meet on the ice → **p. 48**

BEST OF ...

● *A cinema programme to suit everyone*
The *Světozor* two-screen cinema usually shows international films in their original and Czech films with English subtitles → **p. 86**

● *A short lesson in art history*
The interior of the Emmaus monastery – founded in 1347 – is a kaleidoscopic introduction to the history of art. Highlights include a series of Gothic frescoes, plus a bold, reinforced concrete ceiling and twin spires dating from the 20th century. It's a must see! → **p. 104**

● *A game of billiards with a cup of coffee and a cake*
If the weather outside is dismal, then the *Louvre café*, famed for its delicious cakes and five large billiards tables, is just the place to raise the spirits → **p. 66**

● *The beer museum*
Where does that 'liquid gold' come from? All your questions about the Czech Republic's national drink answered in this small museum → **p. 53**

● *The place to shelter in the castle*
If you're in the castle grounds and get caught out by the rain, buy a ticket for the *Vladislav Hall*. The most striking feature here is the rib vaulting, which spans the entire ceiling (photo) → **p. 36**

● *Palladium shopping centre*
Persistent rain can mean only one thing – shopping! There can be no better place to be when it's wet outside. With nearly 200 shops and 30 bars and restaurants, there's something here to suit every taste → **p. 78**

● *Sightseeing by tram*
Tram no. 22 covers nearly all the sights. The National Theatre or Hradčany, the Dancing House or the Rudolfinum – you can see them all from the tram → **p. 47**

RAIN

RELAX AND CHILL OUT
Take it easy and spoil yourself

● *A café with corners and edges*
Prague is renowned for its Cubist architecture. Sit and have a coffee in the *Grand Café* Orient and then have a good look round – you will quickly get to like the style. Everything here from the lamps to the china matches the Cubist exterior and there's a nice atmosphere too → **p. 67**

● *Music at its best*
Take a seat, lean back and enjoy – a concert at the *Rudolfinum* will be of the highest standard and you will come away with fond memories → **p. 86**

● *An island of tranquillity in the Franciscan Garden*
Crowds on Národní třída, traffic fumes on Wenceslas Square – if that's all too much for you, then take a detour to the *Franciscan Garden* and relax in an oasis of green (photo) → **p. 54**

● *The enchanting world of black light theatre*
Theatre without words – ever since 1958, the *Laterna Magika* has been bringing film, dance, mime, music and lighting effects together on to one stage. If you get the chance, buy a ticket. You will be carried away → **p. 91**

● *Relax in the artists' café*
The *Café Montmartre* was a meeting place for artists and writers in the early 20th century. It's only a stone's throw from the Royal Way. Recharge your batteries in the wingback chairs → **p. 66**

● *Steambath in the cellar*
What used to be a torture chamber is now a spa zone. Book a chocolate massage in the Hotel *Hoffmeister's* leisure complex and you will soon forget about its murky past → **p. 94**

● *Take a break with Uncle Joe*
This is a good place to pause for a moment and contemplate the Czech Republic's troubled history. All that is left of the now long demolished monument to Joseph Stalin is the granite base. Give your feet a rest, while enjoying the fine view over the Old Town and the Vltava → **p. 61**

INTRODUCTION

DISCOVER PRAGUE!

'For centuries Prague was an important European city, an intellectual crossroads, a breeding ground for ideas and cultural development' – these were the words used by the former Czech President, Václav Havel, to describe the city where he was born. The fact that after the Velvet Revolution of November 1989 Prague opened itself up again to western Europe and discarded the drab greyness of communism is due in no small part to Václav Havel.

It was especially the complex, sometimes fraught, but also very productive web of relationships between Czechs, Germans and Jews that transformed the Prague of the early 20th century into a cultural crossroads. Writers, such as Franz Kafka, Egon Erwin Kisch and Franz Werfel, epitomise this era. As recently as the 1930s, Prague was a sanctuary for those seeking refuge from the National Socialists, notably German intellectuals, such as Bertolt Brecht and the two brothers, Thomas and Heinrich Mann, as well as opposition Social Democrats, such as Erich Ollenhauer – and that was before flags bearing swastikas started to flutter in Berlin. The fragmentation of

Photo: a view of the Old Town

Czechoslovakia by Hitler's army, World War II, the Holocaust and then the forced expulsion of German speakers after 1945 cruelly ended Prague's reputation as a centre of tolerance and cultural diversity.

Although many Slovaks remained after the partition of Czechoslovakia in 1993 and some moved here to work, the ethnic profile of the capital's population today is largely homogeneous, with almost all of the 1.2 million residents Czech nationals. But what did the city look like 100 years ago when Jews, Germans and Czechs lived side by side? The full story is told in the city's archives, but the clues are there as you wander through the old Jewish quarter of Josefov or when you glimpse the German street names on the Old Town facades.

In the years after the fall of communism, the emergence of an American community caused quite a stir. A large number of college graduates, artists and adventurers came from the U.S. to what they thought was the world capital of the Bohemian lifestyle, a new version of that 19th-century utopia where like-minded people gathered to indulge their particular literary or artistic tastes. So they came in search of inspiration for their first novel, to make a short film or simply to seek their fortune. It is thought that as many as 50,000 Americans lived in Prague during the early 1990s. Today, the city once renowned for its alternative lifestyle is far too expensive and nowhere near exotic enough for an adventure in the 'wild east'. According to statistics, only about 2,500 U.S. citizens live in Prague today. Ukrainians now form the largest minority (almost 35,000), but they

> **Americans came to Prague in pursuit of the Bohemian lifestyle**

One of Prague's famous facades – an Art Nouveau palace on the Old Town Square

play only a small part in the cultural life of the city. Most of them, usually young men, come here to earn money, mainly by working on the building sites. In addition to about 10,000 Russians, there is also a largish Vietnamese community of just under 6,000, many of whom earn a living by selling cheap textiles and vegetables in corner shops. But the Vietnamese are aspirational; they send their children to good schools and are constantly seeking to expand their businesses. Sportisimo, one of the Czech Republic's largest sports goods chains, was founded by two Vietnamese, who came to Prague as students during the communist era.

The majority of the foreigners in Prague today are tourists. On average some 11,000 visitors arrive in the city every day. Backpackers and young people on study tours, coach parties and school groups, families and couples – all lured here by the romantic narrow streets in the Old Town, the pretty corners of the Lesser Town, the majestic Charles Bridge spanning the Vltava and the awe-inspiring juxtaposition of Gothic, Renaissance, Baroque, Art Nouveau and Functionalism. Prague has one of the largest heritage-protected zones in Europe. Almost the whole of the city centre is on UNESCO's list of World Cultural Heritage sites. And rightly so. The Lesser Town and the Old Town merge together to form the brick-and-stone backdrop for an open-air theatre – and quite magnificent it is too!

The people charged with preserving the city's past, with its many different eras and styles, faced a huge challenge. Restoration work began immediately after the fall of communism. With only a few districts where the buildings all date from the same era, the planners are constantly having to ask themselves, what is it that they are actually seeking to protect – a moment in history, uniform rows of houses or individual buildings? When, for example, in the early 1990s, the 'Stone Bell House' on the Old Town Square was renovated, hidden beneath the Baroque facade was the original Gothic stonework. So this beautifully-restored edifice now stands between a splendid Rococo palace and a Renaissance market hall. The renovation work was judged to be exemplary, demonstrating clearly that we must view each building in Prague on its own merits, not necessarily as part of a whole. Now, nearly everything that glitters in the 'Golden City' is once again gold.

Prague was largely spared the bombing of World War II, so slowly but surely the past is coming back to life. A Czech travel guide from the 1960s stated without exaggeration that a visit to Prague is 'the quickest way to understand ten centuries of central European history'. Possibly true, but it has been a long road stained by bloodshed, tragedy and barbarity. One historian summarised the city's past as follows: 'Where in other cities groundwater flows, in Prague it's blood' One particularly violent 'speciality' here was defenestration. The first Prague defenestration took place in 1419. Angry Hussites despatched several Catholic councillors and burghers out of a window in the New Town Hall, an event which was a prelude to the Hussite Wars. The second defenestration of Prague

> **'Where in other cities groundwater flows, in Prague it's blood.'**

was also an expression of the tensions between the two faiths. Angry Protestants threw two Catholic noblemen out of a window in Prague castle. They survived the 16m (50ft) drop because they landed in a medieval dung heap. But this incident marked the start of the Thirty Years' War, a religious war which proved very costly in Czech lives. When in 1648 the Peace of Westphalia was agreed, Bohemia's towns had been destroyed and about half of the inhabitants were dead. Nearly three centuries later, in March 1939, Hitler's troops marched into Prague – World War II with all its atrocities followed shortly after. In August 1968, Warsaw Pact tanks rolled into the city and quelled the 'Prague Spring', thereby destroying any hopes of the 'socialism with a human face' that the Czechs and Slovaks under Alexander Dubček so desperately wanted.

But some positive things did emerge from Prague. In 1348 Charles IV founded the first university in central Europe. By 1600 the court of Rudolf II, which was employing the two astronomers, Johannes Kepler and Tycho Brahe, was a leading centre of learning for the natural sciences. Finally, in November 1989, bloodless mass demonstrations ushered in the Velvet Revolution, leading to the end of communist rule and paving the way for radical social and economic change. Poet president Vaclav Hável was not the only one to dream about Prague once again becoming an 'intellectual crossroads'.

International companies have located to Prague and environs

Since the fall of the Iron Curtain, the lure of the city has increased dramatically – and that means to the business world too. After 1989 foreign investors started looking closely at the 'Golden City'. Practically every international corporation wanted a branch in Prague. A central location in Europe and a reputation for industry and enterprise dating from the early 20th century meant that the Greater Prague region was a highly attractive location – not least for the automotive industry. Today, on the outskirts of Prague, Toyota, Peugeot and Citroen are working together to make a small car, and the famous Škoda brand, now part of the Volkswagen group, has its headquarters near the capital. The IT sector is looking to Prague, the logistics company DHL masterminds its operations from the Czech capital and the German stock market has moved hundreds of jobs to the city. It's true that the average salary in Prague of approx. £900 is still relatively low, but unemployment is close to zero. The economic recovery is continuing, the capital's inhabitants are doing just fine, Prague is booming.

But the boom does bring problems, e.g. every day thousands of cars try to navigate through narrow streets laid out in the Middle Ages for horse-drawn carriages. The mayor of Prague once wearily remarked: 'Other European capitals had decades to solve this sort of problem. We've only had a few years.' According to the latest statistics, almost half the population has a car. Then there are all the commuters who drive into the city from the outskirts. The excellent suburban transport network is mockingly dismissed by many as 'socka', i.e. a mass transit system for the poor. The result: throughout Prague, contractors are digging underground car-parks, excavating tunnels and building bypasses with junctions that eat up the land. So within a period of only a few years, the Prague planners have made precisely the same mistakes as their counterparts in Western Europe. Residents' groups set up to oppose these developments are making only slow progress.

The change from communism to capitalism has happened at a breathtaking pace. Where yesterday there was a corner shop selling groceries, today there's a sushi bar, the down-to-earth pub next door is now an ultra-cool lounge bar, and the old-fashioned

> **For some years now, hypermarkets and shopping malls have been the norm**

café in the Lesser Town is now a Starbucks. Supermarkets no longer suffice. For some years now, hypermarkets and shopping malls have been the norm. Prague continues to expand far beyond the hills beside the Vltava. The urban area covers about 550sq km (210sq mi). More and more satellite towns with smart, detached houses are springing up in Prague's commuter belt. But the estates of dismal, high-rise apartments, which many believed the new regime would want to demolish, live on. They have been modernised and are now resplendent in bright colours.

An excellent public transport system covers the Prague metropolitan area

Fortunately, the prosperity of recent years has not destroyed the city's mystery and magic. When swathes of mist shroud the lanes and alleys of the Old Town, the past seems to overshadow the present. The Czech film director and a native of Prague, Miloš Forman, once called the city a 'seductress with a thousand veils'. It has certainly not lost any of its charms. Prague is a vibrant, modern city where the past is never far away.

WHAT'S HOT

1 Culture clubbing

Entertainment Theatre, music and art come together at the *Meet Factory*, Prague's coolest cultural venue *(Ke Sklárnì 15)*. Equally fashionable is *La Fabrika*. Creative types from around the country either take to the stage or exhibit their work *(Komunardù 30, photo)*. The DJs, gigs and relaxed atmosphere make the *Palais Akropolis (Kubelikova 27)* a popular spot with the younger generation.

Sober

The Eastern European look The Czech capital is noted for its cool fashions. Prague designers pride themselves on their outfits, which are sober, but not plain. Prague's leading figure in the world of fashion is Hana Havelková and she sells her clothes under that name. Her boutique showcases modern classics *(Dušní 10)*. Another top fashion label is *Chi-Chi*, with its sporty, city-friendly look *(www.chi-chi.cz, photo)*. You will find casual, sometimes quirky, styling by local creative folk at *Flamingo Park*. Do take a look at the 'Designer of this Month' *(Truhlářská 29)*!

Dance with me!

Round we go The retro dance trend is spreading. Instead of going to the disco, Prague's youngsters often prefer the ball. A nice dress and a smart dinner jacket are essential requirements at Palác *Žofín* on an island in the Vltava with the same name *(Slovanský ostrov 226)*. If you like the idea of a ball, there's also *Národní důmna Smíchově*, where the music is more contemporary. Classical music and more modern sounds ring out in the Art Nouveau ambience *(Náměstí 14. Října 16)*. If you need to improve your technique, then the place to go is the *Taneční škola Standardklub Praha* (Majerského 2039).

The power of plants

Going organic Prague goes green. Trousers made of hemp, soap from organic olive oil and lavender and delicious sandwiches filled with home-grown vegetables – yes, there's an increasing demand for organic products in Prague. Why not follow the trend? At *Botanicus* you can stock up on lotions, vinegar or candles, all made with ingredients that are grown nearby *(Truhlářská 10)*. You can even buy an 'organic' outfit at *Evergreen*. The clothes they sell are cool *(Uruguayská 6)*! Stop and shop at *Vesmirna*. For organic delicacies served in a relaxed atmosphere *(Ve Smečkách 5, photo)*. If all you want is a snack, go to *Country Life*. The unique selling point at this organic food chain is vegetarian fare at low prices *(Československé armády 30)*.

Karlín calling

A fashionable quarter It used to be a working class district, now it's home to Prague's trendsetters. Karlín has become a centre for arty types and many lively events are staged here. *Karlín Studios* accommodates a dozen or so workshops and galleries *(Křižíkova 34, photo)*. After that, it's on to *Café Touster*, where top DJs perform *(Sokolovská 152)*. If you prefer the sound of guitars, then go to *Abaton*. But you are advised to get tickets in advance, as the gigs here are very popular *(Na kušince 8)*. If you need a pre-drink, then drop in at the *Pivovarsky Klub*. But there's no dance floor. It's a place to eat – and drink. More than 100 types of beer are served in the cellar bar *(Křižíkova 17)*.

IN A NUTSHELL

ARCHITECTURE

Baroque curves, Romanesque arches and Gothic spires, yes, but that does not tell the full story of Prague's architectural grandeur. In amongst them are some outstanding buildings representative of a more modern era. At the start of the 20th century came the nature-inspired ornamentation of Art Nouveau, adopted by many Czech architects, notable examples being the extravagant Municipal House or the old ticket hall in the main station. One architectural style for which Prague is renowned is Cubism with its three-dimensional facades and geometric contrasts. Fine examples of this are the House of the Black Madonna and the first Cubist apartment block *(Bílkova 5)*. The 1920s saw a sober,

unembellished modernity emerging. Czech Radio's headquarters occupies a functional building *(Vinohradská 12)* and sports the typical, angular window lines. The smooth white facades with large windowpanes, as seen on the branches of the Baťa multinational shoe chain, became a trademark (Prague branch: *Wenceslas Square 6)*. Wealthy individuals also loved to push the boundaries. The Brno-born architect, Adolf Loos, built the INSIDER TIP Villa Müller for an entrepreneur. Externally, a simple cube, but step inside the building and you will be struck by its unique room layout with no fixed floors *(Nad hradním vodojemem 14, viewing Tue, Thu, Sat/Sun by appointment, tel. 2 24 31 20 12)*.

During the 1930s, several architects

Photo: The Charles Bridge with the Old Town Bridge Tower on the left

Jazz and Karel Gott, the Prague Spring and the international film scene – the Czech capital has so much to offer

were influenced by the Bauhaus school. This style is clearly evident in the more than 30 residential homes that form the **INSIDER TIP** Baba housing estate on Na ostrohu and Na Babě in the northwest of the city. Post-war socialism left behind a legacy of monstrous, pre-fabricated high-rise apartments on the outskirts of the city, but a handful of imaginative edifices do deserve a mention: the Kotva department store, a reinforced steel structure of juxtaposed hexagonal towers and the 1980s annex to the National Theatre.

This seemingly transparent building with a facade of glass blocks is now home to the famous Laterna Magika theatre company. Sadly, few creative ideas have yet to emerge in the new, post-1989 era. Exceptions are the Dancing House by Frank O. Gehry and Vlado Milunic, and also Jean Nouvel's Zlatý Anděl (Golden Angel) office block.

ATHEISM

Plenty of indisputable evidence testifies to the religious struggles of the

Middle Ages. Around the city centre you will see countless churches with soaring towers and ornate architectural features. And yet Prague is the most secularised of Europe's capitals. Recent censuses reveal that only a quarter of the population consider themselves to be part of a religious community. A newspaper once wrote that the people of Prague would 'rather believe in their horoscope than in god'. Czech godlessness has a tradition that goes back centuries and is usually attributed to forced 'recatholicisation' imposed by the Habsburg rulers. Harassment of the church establishment during the communist era did the rest.

Those you do see will probably be working for a courier service. Hardly anyone thinks of cycling to work. But that's not to do with the city's many hills. First and foremost, cycling in the Czech capital is dangerous. Some of the hazards include potholes in the uneven asphalt, slippery cobblestones and tram tracks. But the main threat to cyclists comes from car drivers. Even so, a few cycling enthusiasts are fighting back. Twice a year, they use the ⊙ *Cyklojízda* to demonstrate that the city does not belong entirely to the car. More and more people are taking part in these pro-cycling 'critical mass' events *(April and September, www.cyklo*

Filming in the heart of the city – by no means an uncommon sight in Prague

CYCLING

When the *víkend* comes, many of Prague's residents collect their mountain bikes from the cellar and head out into the countryside. Cycling is the Czechs' favourite leisure activity. But you will rarely encounter cyclists on the city streets.

jizdy.cz). The campaign is slowly gaining ground. The city authorities are incorporating cycleways when surfaces are repaired or new roads laid. However, it's going to be some time before cycling becomes the norm in Prague. Two wheels is still a dangerous way of getting around.

Just how dangerous will become clear if you happen to be passing the junction of Dukelských hrdinů and nábřeží Kpt. Jaroše near the left bank of the Vltava. An improvised monument, a cycle on a traffic island, commemorates a cycling activist who was run over by a car as he attempted a turn.

DOGS

Small, proud and wilful – the latest statistics show that for the residents of Prague, the dachshund is top dog. But regardless of size, mongrel or pedigree, *retrívr* or *rotvajlr*, dogs are welcome practically everywhere in the Czech capital. In many pubs and bars, waiting staff will happily give patrons' four-legged friends water or titbits. Even at the city police information points, a water bowl is often available. Dogs are cherished and pampered. An estimated 87,000 dogs are registered in the capital, but experts believe that actual numbers are much higher, probably over 100,000. The flip side of a large dog population, of course, lies on the pavement. Small piles of it. Every day, the city's dogs produce several tonnes of poo. In fact, the little fellows are urged to deposit their excrement in special waste bags, which are to be seen everywhere in the city, 'so that you do not have to be ashamed of your dog,' as it says on the bag. But in fact very few use them. So the city's authorities have to send a fleet of 'dog poo mopeds' out on to the streets and they simply hoover up the stinking landmines. And by the way, a Czech dog doesn't go 'woof, woof', but 'haf, haf'.

JAZZ

What sort of music do people associate with Prague? Most would probably say Mozart, Dvořák and jazz. It's true. Jazz has a long tradition here. The communists couldn't do anything about that and so it was tolerated for most of the post-war period. Some top performers, such bassists Miroslav Vitouš and George Mráz and pianist and composer of the 'Miami Vice' soundtrack, Jan Hammer, chose to emigrate to pursue their careers in the USA. For those musicians who stayed at home, jazz became a symbol of civic courage. Many of them ended up in court. And yet the legendary *Reduta* club enjoyed its heyday in the 1960s and 1970s. These were times of experimentation and improvisation. But those heady days are long gone. To be a jazz musician in Prague today, you don't have to be brave, you have to be good. *Pražský jazz* or Prague jazz used to have cult status, but not anymore. The jazz scene is easily accessible. Unambitious mainstream predominates, with the target audience usually tourists, but there are still a few star names. If you see billboards advertising gigs with Jiří Stivín, flute virtuoso, or Milan Svoboda, big-band leader and pianist, then get yourself a ticket. It will be a great experience.

KAREL GOTT

The Czechs respectfully refer to him as 'the master'. Pop icon Karel Gott has been one of the Czech entertainment world's shining stars for decades. He is adored not only at home, but also abroad, especially in Germany and Russia. Year after year he is voted the most popular male singer in the People's Choice Golden Nightingale Award, and in his thank-you speech he always uses the now legendary words: 'I really didn't think I would win it this time'. Most people have forgiven him for supporting the Communist Party hierarchy. When, in 2003, the elected politicians couldn't find a successor to State President Václav Havel, a few rock musicians suggested

Karel Gott. It was meant as a joke, but many people took the idea seriously. So Karel Gott keeps doing what he is best at: singing. He has made more than 100 albums, and has sold at least 30 million records. Female fans were disappointed when in 2008 he married his young girlfriend, Ivana. Even after the birth of his two daughters, the singer (d.o.b. 14.7.1939) is carrying on, true to his principles: 'The best is yet to come'. In fact, he is never afraid to enter new territory. He has a weekly music show on Czech radio – one week he performed a duet with the rapper Bushido singing a cover version of the pop song 'Forever Young'.

Kafka's grave in the New Jewish Cemetery

FRANZ KAFKA

His day job was working as an assessor for a Prague-based workers' accident insurance company. But in his spare time, usually at night, Franz Kafka (1883–1924), the son of a Jewish businessman, wrote a series of remarkable novels in his native language, German. In one of his most famous books, 'The Trial', he describes the turmoil endured by Josef K., who is inexplicably arrested and then passed endlessly between different courts, while in 'Metamorphosis', he shows himself to be a master of the grotesque. For the communist regime, Kafkaesque visions were just a little bit too close to the realities of a totalitarian state and until 1989 the author, who is buried in the New Jewish Cemetery , was persona non grata. For Kafka, Prague was a 'dear little mother with claws'. He had a love-hate relationship with the city of his birth. 'We would have to set fire to it on two sides,' he once wrote. After a long struggle with chronic tuberculosis, Kafka died in a sanatorium near Vienna. He did not marry, was childless and on his death the world was still unaware of his literary talents. Contrary to his express wishes, Kafka's friend, Max Brod, did not burn his manuscripts, thereby bequeathing to posterity a matchless legacy – and to Prague's tourist industry another selling point. In 2003, a rather unusual statue of the man was unveiled in Vězeňská Street near the Spanish Synagogue.

ON LOCATION IN PRAGUE

'Hollywood on the Vltava' – a reputation that Prague has enjoyed since at least 1995, when Tom Cruise arrived in Prague to film 'Mission Impossible'. In the intervening years, international film crews have frequently taken over the capital's maze of narrow lanes and alleys. More recently, scenes Tom Cruise's latest assignment, 'Mission Impossible IV', which premiered in 2011, were shot in Prague. James Bond, alias Daniel Craig, also came here to film 'Casino Royale'. And in the legendary Barrandov Studios, Prague can boast an ultra-modern production centre. Excellent facilities at low prices – that is what makes the Czech 'factory of dreams' so attractive. But of course the historic backdrop plays its part. In 1984, Miloš Forman used locations in the city to shoot 'Amadeus', the story of Mozart. Filmmakers who stayed in the country during the communist regime moved into fairy tales and non-political films for children – and with great success.

Now no-one needs to worry about the censor's pen. The output is mainly low-budget films, but enthusiastic audiences have received the Czech filmworld's work with considerable acclaim. If you want to know exactly who filmed what, where and with whom, then ask at the *Tourist Information Office (Rytířská 31 or in the Old Town Hall)* for the free city map entitled ● INSIDER TIP 'Lights! Camera! Prague!' You can then take a stroll through the city's streets, following in the footsteps of some of Hollywood's greats.

PRAGUE SPRING

Most citizens of Prague think these two words refer to the international music festival of the same name rather than the reform movement of the 1960s. If it hadn't been for the attempt by the communist party leadership under Alexander Dubček to give socialism in Czechoslovakia a human face, then the history of the eastern bloc may have followed a different course. Dubček fell out with his masters in Moscow, when he dropped the rules on censorship at home and then,

in his foreign policy, forged links with the West. After several warnings, on 21 August 1968 Warsaw Pact countries

Weekend is when everyone gets out on their bikes

marched into Czechoslovakia and ended the Prague Spring, ushering in an Ice Age that was to last 21 years. Moscow took the line that the invasion was to prevent a civil war. The West held back from any intervention for fear of triggering a superpower confrontation. Alexander Dubček, who died in 1992, was expelled from the Communist Party in 1970 and then worked in the forestry service in what is now Slovakia. Many intellectuals went into exile in the West.

THE PERFECT DAY
Prague in 24 hours

09:00am SURVEY THE SCENE

First of all, you need to get an overview. So take the funicular railway, dating from 1891, from the Lesser Town. Within only a few minutes, you will be at the top of *Petřín* → p. 104. The Old Town, the Lesser Town and the Vltava are down below, while Hradčany beckons on the left (photo left).

10:00am ON THE CASTLE MOUND

Now head downhill on foot passing the *Strahov monastery* → p. 32 and make for *Hradčany* → p. 28. Pass through the gateway guarded by the Ignaz Platzer's gargantuan 'Battling Titans' and enter the vast complex, now the seat of the Czech president. As you stroll through the site, make sure you include in your itinerary these two highlights: look inside *St Vitus Cathedral* → p. 34 and then wander down the *Golden Lane* → p. 31.

12:00pm DESCEND ON THE ROYAL WAY

You will save energy if you follow the route the king took on the day of his coronation, but in the reverse direction. Today the *Royal Way* → p. 26 is a well-trodden tourist route – but it's still something you just have to do! Simply ignore all the souvenir shops and marvel at the fine array of palaces and town houses along the Nerudova.

01:00pm FORTIFY YOURSELF WITH DUMPLINGS

No visit to Prague is complete without a plate of dumplings. Classic Bohemian dishes are always on the menu in the *Malostranská beseda* → p. 69. But if you're looking for something a little lighter, don't worry. It's not all stodgy fare. And while you're eating, you can sit and watch the non-stop action on the Malostranské náměstí.

02:00pm OVER THE RIVER

A walk across the *Charles Bridge* → p. 47, the oldest and most famous of the Vltava crossings, is of course an absolute must. Are you keen to get away from the crowds of tourists and feeling fit? If so, then leave the bridge just beyond the western bridge tower via a flight of steps. A detour will take you from here on to the pretty peninsula known as the *Kampa* → p. 38 (photo centre). Some parts of it are reminiscent of Venice.

Get to see the best of Prague – be at the heart of things, no rush and all in a day

`03:00pm` THE OLD TOWN AND THE JEWISH QUARTER

On the Old Town side the Royal Way is called Karlova. Eventually, the narrow streets open out and before long you are standing on the *Old Town Square* → p. 45, Prague's finest plaza. Just beyond it is *Josefov* → p. 41. As you stand and survey the jumble of gravestones in the *cemetery* → p. 42, you will be looking back at over 1,000 years of Jewish history. Do take a look inside the *Pinkasova Synagogue* → p. 49, the *Spanish Synagogue* → p. 51 and also the *Old-New Synagogue* → p. 44 (photo right), where it is said the legendary golem once resided.

`05:00pm` COFFEE WITH A VIEW

If it's time for a break, then take a tram (no. 17 or 18) along the banks of the Vltava to the famous *Café Slavia* → p. 67. It has a number of plus points: delicious food, a distinctive Art Deco interior and large windows, through which you get a clear view of the National Theatre, Hradčany and the Vltava quayside.

`06:00pm` SHOPPING 'ON THE MOAT'

By now, you will be thinking of gifts and souvenirs. There are no better places for this than *Národní trída (National Avenue)* and *Na příkopě* (literally 'on the moat') → p. 74. Both come into the category of 'shopping heaven'.

`07:30pm` CLASSICAL MUSIC AND MORE

A concert by the Prague Symphony Orchestra (FOK) in the *Municipal House* → p. 50 is not just only a musical experience par excellence, but the splendour of the Art Nouveau interior will overwhelm you. If you're keen on opera, you should get tickets for the *Estates Theatre* → p. 51, where the première of Mozart's 'Don Giovanni' was performed. If there's still time, sit in style in the *Monarch wine bar* → p. 84 and enjoy a well-deserved drink.

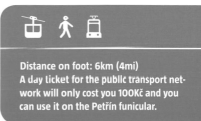

Distance on foot: 6km (4mi)
A day ticket for the public transport network will only cost you 100Kč and you can use it on the Petřín funicular.

SIGHTSEEING

CITY **WHERE TO START?**
It has to be the **Royal Way**. On their coronation day, kings used to walk from the Powder Tower **(128 C4)** *(ⓜ G–H4)* via the Old Town Square and the Charles Bridge up to the castle **(126 B4)** *(ⓜ D3)*. This is exactly the same route the tourists take today and it passes all the main sights. Good footwear is essential, because you will have no recourse to public transport or your own car. In fact, you might as well leave your car in the hotel carpark. There is hardly any free parking in the city centre.

Even Mozart was struck by Prague's diversity. In 1791 he remarked: 'Every day I take the same route home and every time I see something new'. These words are just as true today. Visitors and locals alike marvel when the newly restored facades are revealed; buildings are often hidden by scaffolding for months.

And even in places where the renovation work was completed long ago, there's always something changing – especially in the city centre. Where a year before there was a bakery, there's now a boutique, or a hairdressing salon has been transformed into a fashionable café. Now more than two decades since what became known as the Velvet Revolution, Prague is still in a state of flux. On the other hand, the magnificent, historic heart of the city to

Photo: St Vitus Cathedral in the Castle Quarter

Dancing houses, golden lanes and an old new town – at every corner of the Czech capital there are many fascinating sights to behold

the left and right of the Vltava River has hardly changed. During World War II, Prague was largely spared from aerial bombing. The warm words of another regular visitor to Prague, Thomas Mann, are also just as valid today: 'I'm so glad to be back here in this city whose architectural charm is, among all the cities in the world, almost unique'.

A fascination for the city has gripped millions of tourists from all over the world – backpackers, short-break tourists, school parties and study groups. There is no low season to speak of, so even in winter you will find you have plenty of company on the Charles Bridge. If you want to enjoy the famous river crossing in peace, then you will have to come early in the morning or late in the afternoon. The same goes for the city's second symbol, Prague Castle. It is also worthwhile deviating from the well-trodden route of the Royal Way (from the Powder Tower up to the Castle) to explore the surrounding maze of alleyways well away from the throngs of tourists.

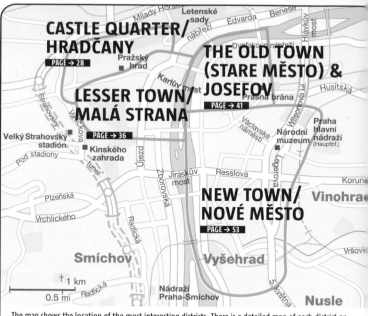

The map shows the location of the most interesting districts. There is a detailed map of each district on which each of the sights described is numbered.

If a walk through this 'open-air museum' is not enough, there are plenty of other museums to explore – but remember that most of them are closed on Monday. Admission prices to most museums and galleries are significantly lower than in many other countries. This is not a generous gesture to tourists, more respect for the fact that many Czechs take a keen interest in their own culture and their income is generally lower than that of most western Europeans. Unfortunately, some museums only provide explanatory texts for the exhibits in the Czech language. If this is the case, then you can always call on the services of a tour guide provided either by the Prague Information Service *(PIS, Staroměstské náměstí 1 | tel. 2 21 71 44 44 | tourinfo@pis.cz)* or other organisations.

CASTLE QUARTER/ HRADČANY

MAP INSIDE BACK COVER

★ *Hradčany* is the largest castle complex in the world, and yet at busy times it seems to be too small for the many visitors.

Every year about 1 million tourists flock to this imposing site perched on a hill about 70m (230ft) above the city. Once the residence of Bohemian princes and kings, Prague Castle has been the seat of the head of state since 1918.

Its present appearance is attributable

mainly to the reign of the Habsburg empress, Maria Theresa, who commissioned a full-scale renovation in the second half of the 18th century. The first fortress on the site can be traced back to the 9th century. Over the centuries, new fortifications, palaces, churches and administrative buildings were added, burnt down and in many cases rebuilt. Today Prague Castle with its three courtyards consists of around 60 separate buildings. Its first heyday occurred during the rule of Emperor Charles IV (1316–1378), whose main achievements included the laying of the foundation stone for St Vitus Cathedral in 1344. Another highpoint in its history came under Rudolf II (1576–1612). He brought together distinguished scientists, artists and alchemists and amassed a huge collection of curiosities.

After the founding of Czechoslovakia in 1918, President Tomáš Garrigue Masaryk arranged for an 'artistic upgrade' of his official residence. The task was undertaken by the Slovenian architect, Jože Plečnik. Soon after he became president in 1989, Václav Havel decided to make some visible changes to the castle. He gave the job of redesigning parts of the interior and the copper-adorned entrance portals to the presidential chancellery in the second courtyard to his friend, the glass artist, Bořek Šípek. In 1990 at Havel's request, Oscar winner Theodor Píštěk, the costume designer for Miloš Forman's famous film ‹Amadeus›, created new uniforms for the castle guards. The ● INSIDER TIP Changing of the Guard, which takes place every day at noon at the *Castle Gate* (126 B4) (*D3*), is a spectacle worth seeing and hearing… and it is an event that is accessible to everyone for free.

If you visit the castle complex, do make a point of touring the surrounding area. Hradčany, the castle district, was established in 1320. Charles IV enlarged the area around the *Strahov Monastery* with its famous library, parts of *Petřín hill* and

⭐ **Hradčany**
The country's political and intellectual centre
→ p. 28

⭐ **Golden Lane**
Eleven tiny houses shrouded in legend
→ p. 31

⭐ **Kampa**
Attractive peninsula with just a hint of Venice → p. 38

⭐ **Old Jewish Cemetery**
Memorial to a lost world → p. 42

⭐ **Old-New Synagogue**
According to legend, the golem once resided here and its lifeless remains are lying in the synagogue's attic → p. 44

⭐ **Old Town Square**
The Astronomical Clock and an array of fine facades → p. 45

⭐ **Charles Bridge**
Sixteen piers support an avenue of Baroque statues over the romantic Vltava → p. 47

⭐ **Vyšehrad**
A bizarre rock formation beside the Vltava with a church, a famous cemetery and a magnificent view → p. 59

⭐ **Wenceslas Square**
This bustling boulevard has witnessed some epic political struggles → p. 59

⭐ **A collection of modern art**
A stunning array of artworks by the Masters → p. 61

MARCO POLO HIGHLIGHTS

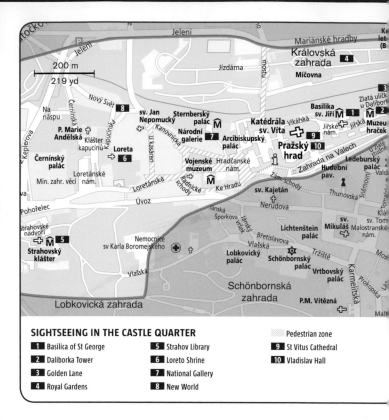

SIGHTSEEING IN THE CASTLE QUARTER

- **1** Basilica of St George
- **2** Daliborka Tower
- **3** Golden Lane
- **4** Royal Gardens
- **5** Strahov Library
- **6** Loreto Shrine
- **7** National Gallery
- **8** New World
- **9** St Vitus Cathedral
- **10** Vladislav Hall

▨▨▨ Pedestrian zone

the district of *Pohořelec*. To get away from the tourist crowds, take a stroll through the pretty streets of the *New World (Nový Svět)*. Artists and intellectuals once lived in the small cottages here, because rents were low. The buildings have been renovated, the rents are no longer low, but this little corner of Hradčany still evokes the romance of a bygone age. *Castle complex April–Oct daily 5am–midnight, Nov–March 6am–11pm | admission free | buildings and Golden Lane April–Oct daily 9am–6pm, Nov–March 9am–4pm | admission 250–350Kč (depending on type of tour) | some gardens closed in winter | tram 22: Pražský hrad*

1 BASILICA OF ST GEORGE
(126 C4) (*Ⓜ E3*)

The reddish facade of the basilica is not very inviting, but the late Baroque *double staircase* and the Romanesque *choir inside* more than compensate. Rebuilt in 1150 after a fire, this church is regarded as the finest Romanesque church in the Czech capital. It was consecrated in 925 as the burial church for St Wenceslas' grandmother, St Ludmila. Her final resting place is located in the *chapel* south of the choir. In front of the crypt lie the tombs of the Přemyslid rulers, Vratislav (died 921) and Boleslav II (died 999). The Renaissance columned portal was the work of the German architect, Benedikt Ried, and dates from the 16th century. In the apse you can see the remains of a *ceiling fresco*, entitled 'Heavenly Jerusalem', which was created around 1200. The neighbouring Benedictine monastery dates from 973. It now houses a permanent exhibition entitled the 'Early Art of Bohemia'. *April–Oct daily 9am–6pm, Nov–March 9am–4pm | admission with castle ticket from 250Kč*

▓2 DALIBORKA TOWER
(126 C4) (*ŒŒ E3*)

The tower was part of a late-Gothic fortification dating from the 15th century, and until the 18th century was a prison. It bears the name of the first prisoner, Dalibor, the knight of Kozojedy. It is said that this leader of a peasant uprising played his fiddle so beautifully here until his execution in 1498 that every day passers-by stopped to listen and to supply him with food. Four centuries later, Smetana used the legend as the basis for his opera, 'Dalibor'. The work was played at the ceremonial laying of the foundation stone for the National Theatre in 1868. *April–Oct daily 9am–6pm, Nov–March 9am–4pm | admission with castle ticket from 250Kč*

▓3 GOLDEN LANE (ZLATÁ ULIČKA)
★ (126 C3–4) (*ŒŒ E3*)

Prague tourist office reckons that on many days more people visit this narrow alley than cross the Charles Bridge. To restrict the flow of tourists, an admission charge is made at the main opening times. So try to remember: if you come ● INSIDERTIP after 4pm (Nov–March) or 6pm (April–Oct), you can view Prague's most famous street until the castle area closes at 11pm or midnight, not only at no charge, but also without all the crowds. The only gold that has ever been produced here was the literary treasure that flowed from the pen of Franz Kafka. For several months in 1916 he lived at the much-visited no. 22. However, no alchemists ever lived in any of the small 16th-century cottages – even if legend has it that they were accommodated here by

Nothing glittering in Golden Lane today, but some fine old houses to admire

Library in the Strahov Monastery – a place for pleasure or for study

Rudolf II and given the task of making gold! In fact, castle guards and poor artisans lived here. *April–Oct daily 9am–6pm, Nov–March 9am–4pm | admission with castle ticket from 250Kč*

◪ ROYAL GARDEN (KRÁLOVSKÁ ZAHRADA) (126 B–C3) (*Ⓜ D–E3*)

The renowned master gardener Francesco, from Italy, created this area in 1534 to a plan drawn up by the architect, Giovanni Spatio. This was the first Italianate garden in Bohemia. Between 1555 and 1558 Prague horticulturalists extended the site. Shortly after it was redesigned in Dutch style by Jan de Vries Vredeman. In the second half of the 17th century, the garden was laid out in its present form as a French Baroque park. The statue 'Allegory of Night', in front of the Ball Game Hall with its sgraffito decoration, was probably the work of Matthias Braun. At the end of the garden stands the *Belveder Summer Palace*, a fine example of mid-16th century, Italian Renaissance architecture. King Ferdinand I built it for his wife, Anna. *April/Oct 10am–6pm, May/Sept 10am–7pm, June/July 10am–9pm, Aug 10am–8pm | tram 22: Pražský hrad*

▣ STRAHOV LIBRARY (STRAHOVSKÁ KNIHOVNA) (126 A5) (*Ⓜ C4*)

What did Franz Kafka write to his parents one day before his death? The Museum of Czech Literature keeps this letter from 1924, along with thousands of other documents. It safeguards the legacy of famous Czech authors, and not just Franz Kafka, but also Egon Erwin Kisch and many others. Such papers are invaluable to students of literature. The museum is only a small part of the once powerful Premonstratensian monastery, in which the most interesting room is almost certainly the Theological Hall with its Baroque bookcases filled with old books, antique globes and adorned with stunning ceiling frescoes. Despite considerable war damage, the Strahov Monastery, which was rebuilt several times, has lost none of its grandeur. It was founded by Prince Vladislav II in 1140. ☀ Wander just a short distance from the site and you will be rewarded with some fine views over Prague. *Daily 9am–noon, 1pm–5pm | 80Kč | Strahovské nádvoří 1 | www.strahovskyklaster.cz | tram 22: Pohořelec*

6 LORETO SHRINE (LORETA)
(126 A4) (*C–D3*)

Italian visitors are often taken aback when they visit this site, which dates from between 1626 and 1631. Is not exactly the same shrine to be found near the Adriatic town of Ancona? Correct! The Prague complex is a replica. It was originally, or so it is said, the 'Casa Santa', the house in Nazareth where the Virgin Mary lived. According to the legend, angels carried the house from Palestine to the Loreta laurel plantation near Ancona. So, not surprisingly, Princess Lobkowitz chose two Italians, Giovanni Orsi and Andrea Allio, to build the reproduction. One particularly impressive feature is the Casa's *two-storey* cloister – the second floor (1740) was the work of Kilian Ignaz Dientzenhofer. Twenty years previously he had designed the facade and the *bell tower*. On the hour, 'We Greet Thee a Thousand Times', a hymn praising the Virgin Mary, rings out from its 27 Dutch bells. Inside the Casa, do take a look at the *Madonna* carved from the wood of a linden tree. Another interesting sight is the curious 'Chapel of Our Lady of the Sorrows'. Legend has it that, by divine intervention, a Portuguese princess sprouted a bushy beard, so that men would no longer find her attractive. Far more attractive and the highlight of the exhibition is the INSIDER TIP *Monstrance*, which is studded with 6,222 diamonds. Weighing 12kg (25lb) and 90cm (3ft) in height, it was made in Vienna in 1698/99. *Daily Nov–March 9.30am–12.15pm, 1pm–4pm, April–Oct 9am–12.15pm, 1pm–5pm | 110Kč | Loretánské náměstí 7 | www.loreta.cz | tram 22: Pohořelec*

BOOKS & FILMS

▶ **The Trial** was written by Franz Kafka in 1915 and tells the story of Josef K, who is arrested and prosecuted by the authorities, but does not know what offence he has committed.

▶ **I Served the King of England** is a novel by Bohumil Hrabal set in Prague in the 1940s. It follows the fortunes of antihero, Díte, during the war and the troubled times thereafter. Although written in the 1970s, it was not published until 1983. It was made into a film with the same title (2006). Hrabal also wrote the story behind **Closely Observed Trains**, a much-admired film directed by Jiří Menzel (1966).

▶ **City, Sister, Silver** by Jáchym Topol and published in 2000 examines the feelings of the younger generation during and after the Velvet Revolution

▶ Although he trained in Prague as a film director in the late 1940s, Milan Kundera (b. 1929) is probably best known for his contribution to modern Czech literature. **The Unbearable Lightness of Being** (1984) is his most famous work. It was made into a film in 1988.

▶ **Kolya** (1996) – A middle-aged musician from Prague, who is a dedicated bachelor, finds himself caring for a young Russian boy. The two slowly get to know each other and in the autumn of 1989 experience the Velvet Revolution together. Directed by Jan Svěrák and starring his father, Zdeněk Svěrák, the film won a number of awards.

🟥7 NATIONAL GALLERY (NÁRODNÍ GALLERY) (126 B4) (𝕸 D3)

The Sternberg Palace, built around 1700 to designs by Domenico Martinelli and Giovanni Battista Alliprandi, houses a vast collection of works by German, Italian and Flemish artists. One highlight is Albrecht Dürer's 'Feast of the Rosary'; it was painted in Venice in 1506. Dürer is himself immortalised in this picture, which Emperor Rudolf II acquired and then arranged for it to be brought on foot across the Alps to Prague.

Also impressive is Jan Gossaert's 'Madonna with St Luke', the evangelist being depicted in a deferential pose. The gallery also showcases an unspectacular but carefully selected collection of works by Lucas Cranach the Elder, El Greco, Francisco Goya, Frans Hals, Rembrandt, Peter Paul Rubens and Tintoretto. Other masterpieces in the collection include Russian icons and works by Italian masters of the 14th and 15th centuries. *Tue–Sun 10am–6pm | 150Kč | Hradčanské náměstí 15 | www.ngprague.cz | tram 22: Pražský hrad*

LOW BUDGET

▶ It's cheaper and much more fun than the usual sightseeing boat trip – rent a pedalo or rowing boat on the banks of the Žofín peninsula *(access via Masarykovo nábřeží | 10am until sunset | ca. 250Kč/per hr)*. Pedal or row your way round the *Střelecký ostrov* **(128 A5–6)** *(𝕸 F5)*, an island in the Vltava, and you will gain a whole new perspective on the Old Town, the Lesser Town and the Charles Bridge.

▶ Every day at 11am (in summer also at 2pm), a free guided tour in English starts at the corner of *Old Town Square/Pařížská* **(128 B4)** *(𝕸 G4)*. The guides are usually Czech students. They make their money from tips. *www.newpraguetours.com*

▶ You can buy a 3-day ticket costing 400Kč that will give you admission to the *National Museum* and all other associated institutions *(the Smetana Museum, the Dvořák Museum, the Music Museum, the Lapidarium and the monument on Vítkov Hill)*.

🟥8 INSIDER TIP NEW WORLD (NOVÝ SVĚT) (126 A4) (𝕸 C3)

Situated quite close to the Loreto Shrine is this picturesque quarter, which dates from the 16th century. The cottages, many of which are now used as artists' studios, were smartened up in the 18th century. Decades ago, the *Golden Pear* (no. 3) was a tavern for workers, now it is an upmarket restaurant. Around 1600, Tycho Brahe, the Danish astronomer and an important figure at Emperor Rudolf II's court, lived at no. 1. During the 1960s, the New World district was the creative headquarters for 'Pan Tau' director, Jindrich Polak. *Metro: Hradčanská (A), tram 22: Pohořelec*

🟥9 ST VITUS CATHEDRAL (126 C4) (𝕸 D3)

The 96m (315ft) twin towers of St Vitus Cathedral proclaim to the world that the castle was not just a secular power base, but also a dominant force in the ecclesiastical world. But since its expropriation by the Communist government, this Gothic edifice no longer belongs to the Catholic Church. And the many years of legal wrangling after the political upheavals of the 1980s changed nothing. In the end in 2010 church and state agreed that they would share responsibility for this 'national symbol'. Strangely, the people of what is Europe's most atheist nation regard the church as a national treasure. Not only is the great Bohemian king, Charles IV, buried here, but also his most illustrious

porary, but it has never been replaced. Under Parler's plans there was no provision for stained glass windows, but the huge, kaleidoscopic *rose window* entitled the 'Creation of the World' over

St Vitus Cathedral – the west front with its huge rose window

successors, so it is an important historical symbol for the Czech people.

The story of the cathedral began in 1344, but it did not end until 1929. The first architect, Matthew of Arras, was appointed by Charles IV. After the Frenchman's death in 1352, Peter Parler, then a 23-year-old architect who had worked on Cologne cathedral, was commissioned to continue with the work. In the following 46 years he completed the south transept and the choir. After Parler's death in 1399, resources were devoted to the Hussite Wars and it was not until 1892 that the two 82-m (270-ft) high *west towers* were completed. The nearly 100-m (325-ft) high main tower was begun in Gothic, continued in Renaissance and finished in Baroque style. The slightly unorthodox copper pinnacle was intended to be tem-

the west door covers an area of 100sq m (1,050sq ft). Although quite out of keeping with Parler's original concept, the overall effect is quite breathtaking. The 27,000 fragments of coloured glass were assembled by František Kysela in 1921. Another remarkable feature is the INSIDER TIP Cyril and Methodius window in the third chapel. Commissioned by a bank, it is the work of the Art Nouveau artist, Alfons Mucha.

One highly-prized treasure in the St Wenceslas Chapel is stored beside the south portal: the *Bohemian Crown Jewels*. Only on rare occasions are they exhibited (most recently in 2008, again provisionally in 2013). The door to the coronation chamber is secured by seven locks, with each key kept by seven different people, including the President, the Archbishop of Prague and the mayor. *Cathedral/bell-tower April–Oct Mon–Sat 9am–5pm, Sun noon–5pm, Nov–March Mon–Sat 9am–4pm, Sun noon–4pm | admission to the front area free; you need a castle ticket for the rear area from 250Kč*

🔟 VLADISLAV HALL ●
(126 C4) (*ⁿⁿ E3*)

Some 62m (200ft) long, 16m (50ft) wide and 13m (40ft) high, the Vladislav Hall (also called the Tribute Room) occupies the second floor of the former Royal Palace. Completed in 1502, it is where Bohemian kings were elected, and since 1918 every state president has been sworn into office beneath the late Gothic vaulting. But it has not always been a testament to democracy. During the Late Middle Ages banquets and tournaments were held in the Vladislav Hall. Knights on horseback descended the riders' staircase with its wide, shallow steps, which now form the exit in the north wing. In the room next to the hall you will find the castle's most

famous window. In 1618 two governors appointed by the Habsburg emperor were hurled out of the window and into the ditch below. The so-called Second Defenestration of Prague sparked the Thirty Years' War between Protestants and Catholics, which developed into a power struggle throughout Europe. *April–Oct daily 9am–6pm, Nov–March 9am–4pm | admission with castle ticket from 250Kč*

LESSER TOWN/MALÁ STRANA

Probably Prague's prettiest quarter is to be found below Hradčany. Malà Strana means 'little quarter', but it is often translated as the 'Lesser Town'. Filmmakers love it. All they have to do is to remove the cars and dismantle the advertisements and they have the perfect backdrop for a scene straight out of the 18th century.

And the residents of Prague are very fond of the district too, not least because of its many green open spaces. In 1257 the Přemyslid king, Otakar II, granted the 17-acre site, at that time known as the 'new town under the castle' or 'smaller Prague town', full municipal rights. During the 16th century proximity to the centre of power, i.e. the castle, led to a building boom driven by the nobility. The burgers grew rich from the steady business that the royal court provided. Huge mansions in Renaissance and Baroque style were built. Nowadays the locals are drawn to the quarter because of the relaxing atmosphere in the many parks and gardens. If you want to escape the traffic noise on the *Letenská*, it's so easy – just step inside the high walls of the *Wallenstein Garden*.

Wallenstein Garden

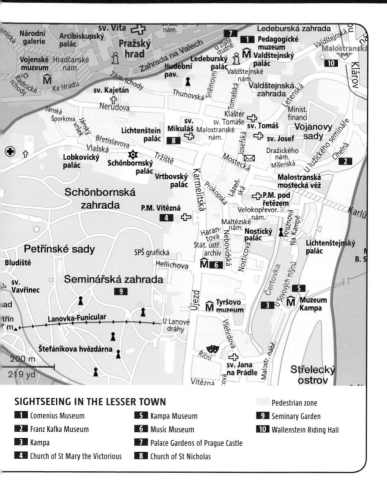

SIGHTSEEING IN THE LESSER TOWN

- **1** Comenius Museum
- **2** Franz Kafka Museum
- **3** Kampa
- **4** Church of St Mary the Victorious
- **5** Kampa Museum
- **6** Music Museum
- **7** Palace Gardens of Prague Castle
- **8** Church of St Nicholas
- **9** Seminary Garden
- **10** Wallenstein Riding Hall

Pedestrian zone

A popular destination for a Sunday stroll is the *Kampa* peninsula between the Vltava and the narrow Čertovka. And whatever the time of year, do go up *Petřín*. There's a magnificent view over the city from the top of this hill, an ever-present feature on the Prague skyline. Nature has bestowed many favourable assets on the quarter, but when in the August of 2002 Prague experienced its worst floods for 500 years, the Lesser Town suffered the most. However, unlike other parts of the city, it recovered very quickly from the flood damage, partly because the medieval architects had designed the buildings so solidly that they are capable of withstanding the regular high waters. Now few local people live in the historic houses. Countless foreign embassies, the two chambers of the Czech parliament and the machinery of state have taken over most of the real estate. Anything

A picturesque spot – the Kampa peninsula

else has been renovated and turned into offices or boutique hotels. And yet, if in the evening you take a walk through the streets of the Lesser Town, illuminated only by dimly-lit lanterns, you will quickly realise that the past is sometimes more alive than the present.

■1 COMENIUS MUSEUM (PEDAGOGICKÉ MUZEUM J. A. KOMENSKÉHO) (126 C4) *(ω E3)*

The House of the Golden Sun *(U zlatého slunce)* is dedicated to the life and work of Jan Amos Comenius (1592–1670). The teacher and preacher was the last bishop of the Brethren of Bohemia and Moravia. He developed an enlightened approach to pedagogy and is now universally acknowledged as the father of modern education. *Tue–Sun 10am–12.30 and 1pm–5pm | 60Kč | Valdštejnská 20 | metro: Malostranská (A)*

■2 FRANZ KAFKA MUSEUM ● (128 A4) *(ω E4)*

These rooms, opened in 2005 courtesy of a private initiative, are situated on the Lesser Town banks of the Vltava. They explore at various levels the relationship between the writer and his home town of Prague. The man behind the design of the exhibition is the Argentinian artist, Juan Insua, who wanted to create in word, image, light and music a 'symphonic whole'. *Daily 10am–6pm | 180Kč | Cihelná 2b | www. kafkamuseum.cz | metro: Malostranská (A)*

■3 KAMPA ★ (127 D5) *(ω E4)*

This attractive riverside strip of land is popular with strollers. Separating the Vltava from the Lesser Town is an artificial channel called the *Čertovka* or Devil's Stream. For centuries, the fast-flowing water powered mill wheels. At the northern end of Kampa is the district known as *Prague's Venice (Pražské Benátky)*, a cluster of old houses. Originally Kampa was just gardens, but then mills took over the banks to take advantage of the water-power. The first one, the *Sova Mill (Sovovy mlýny)* dates from the 13th century. It was re-opened as a museum in 2003. The townhouses on the Kampa date from the 16th century. *Metro: Malostranská (A)*

4 CHURCH OF ST MARY THE VICTORIOUS (KOSTEL PANNY MARIE VÍTĚZNÉ) (126 C5) (⊞ E4)

Built in 1611 to replace a Hussite church, this was the first Baroque structure of its kind in Prague. Originally it was German Lutherans who worshipped here, but in 1624 during the Counter-Reformation it fell into the hands of the Catholic Carmelite Order. A destination for pilgrims from all over the world is the wax figure of the INSIDER TIP *Infant Jesus of Prague*, a Spanish Renaissance work of 1628. When Pope Benedict came to the Czech capital in 2009, he donated a golden crown, which he placed on the head of the revered statuette. *Mon–Sat 9.30am–7pm, Sun 8.30am–8pm | Karmelitská 9 | tram 12, 20, 22: Hellichova*

5 KAMPA MUSEUM (MUZEUM KAMPA) (127 D5) (⊞ E4)

This stylish museum, opened in 2003 and dedicated to the art collection of the Czech exile Meda Mládková, is situated beside the Vltava in a renovated mill *(Sovovy mlýny)*, which dates from the 14th century. It houses a unique collection of modern art from central Europe, for example, works by Otto Gutfreund and Frantisek Kupka, as well as pieces from the communist era. There's also a restaurant and an interesting ↘ glass viewing platform. *Daily 10am–6pm | 280Kč | Kampa island | www.museumkampa.cz | tram 9, 12, 20, 22: Újezd*

6 INSIDER TIP MUSIC MUSEUM (ČESKÉ MUZEUM HUDBY) (126 C5) (⊞ E4)

This amazing Baroque palace dating from the 17th century displays a collection of musical instruments and documents, some more than 500 years old. One particular highlight is an original score by Mozart. Curios include a collection of guitar replicas from the communist era and interesting array of historic keyboard instruments. Modern audio-visual methods are used to showcase the exhibits in the 'Man–Instrument–Music' section. What adds to the museum's appeal is the fact that you can hear the musical instruments being played at listening posts in each room. *Mon 1pm–6pm, Wed 10am–8pm, Thu–Sun 10am–6pm | 60Kč | Karmelitská 2 | tram 12, 20, 22: Hellichova*

7 PALACE GARDENS OF PRAGUE CASTLE (PALÁCOVÉ ZAHRADY) (126 C4) (⊞ E3)

Nestling on the castle hill in a delightful spot are these terraced gardens, which at one time belonged to the Ledebour, Fürstenberg and Kolowrat dynasties. Striking features include balustrades, staircases and fountains. The Kolowrat Garden is considered to be the finest spot in Malá Strana; it was laid out in Rococo style around 1784 by Ignác Palliardi. From 1923 until the outbreak of war the adjoining palace was the seat of Czechoslovakia's democratic government. The Ledebour Garden was also designed by Palliardi (1787). A foundation, whose patrons included Prince Charles and Vaclav Havel, the Czech Republic's former president who died in 2011, was responsible for renovating this pretty site. It is not known who was responsible for the Fürstenberg Garden. The palace is now the seat of the Polish Embassy. *April/Oct 10am–6pm, May/Sept 10am–7pm, June/July 10am–9pm, Aug 10am–8pm | 80Kč | Valdstejnske Square 3 | metro: Malostranská (A)*

8 CHURCH OF ST NICHOLAS (CHRÁM SV. MIKULÁŠE) (126 C4) (⊞ E4)

It's simply breathtaking. So vast is the Baroque Church of St Nicholas, built in the Lesser Town by Christoph Dientzenhofer and son Kilian Ignaz between 1703 and 1756, that there would be room inside it for the 60-m (200-ft) high observation tower at the top of Petřín. The facade (1710) is a masterpiece of Bohemian Baroque. When Johann Lukas Kracker was painting the *fresco* in 1760 above the 75-m (250-ft) high nave, every day dozens of Prague citizens came to watch

303 steps to the viewing platform, the reward is a ☆ stunning view over the city. *Church: March–Oct daily 9am–5pm, Nov–Feb 9am–4pm, admission: 70Kč; Tower: daily 10am–6pm, March/Oct until 8pm, July/Sept until 10pm, admission: 100Kč | Malostranské náměstí | metro: Malostranská (A)*

High Baroque – the huge St Nicholas Church

the spectacle. The 'Apotheosis of St Nicholas', which covers an area of 150sq m (1600sq ft), is one of Europe's largest paintings. Franz Xaver Balko painted the Holy Trinity fresco in the dome, while the four oversized figures beneath it were the work of the Rococo sculptor, Ignaz Platzer. The almost 80-m (260-ft) **INSIDER TIP** high belltower was designed by y Anselmo Lurago. During the communist era, agents belonging to the Czechoslovak secret service used the tower as a lookout point. Within sight in the Lesser Town were many Western embassies. A small exhibition houses binoculars and other photographic apparatus used by the inquisitive observers. If you climb the

9 ■ **SEMINARY GARDEN (SEMINÁŘSKÁ ZAHRADA)** (126 B–C5) (*Ⰳ D–E4*)
The garden was laid out in the mid-17th century for the Carmelite Order resident at St Mary the Victorious Church. It did not acquire its present name until the end of the 18th century, when it became part of the Episcopal Seminary. Today the garden is a popular place for strollers, particularly in the spring. Once the blossom comes out, painters and photographers move on to the slope in force, pushchairs and young children invade the manicured lawns, dogs chase each other in a frenzy and young lovers gaze adoringly at each other on the benches. *Tram 12, 20, 22: Hellichova*

10 **WALLENSTEIN RIDING HALL (VALDŠTEJNSKÁ JÍZDÁRNA)**

(127 D4) *(∅ E3)*

In the tastefully converted stables that once belonged to the Wallenstein family, the National Gallery stages temporary exhibitions of fine art and photography. The number of visitors to this museum in the park next to Malostranská metro station does occasionally exceed its capacity. Before the former riding hall was converted into an exhibition hall during the 1950s, it was used as a repair workshop by vehicle manufacturers Laurin & Klement, which later became the now famous Škoda company. *Tue–Sun 10am–6pm | 150Kč | Valdštejnská 3 | metro: Malostranská (A)*

THE OLD TOWN (STARÉ MĚSTO) & JOSEFOV

The 'Old Town' has always been one of Prague's liveliest districts. This quarter has seen constant change ever since the 10th century, when the first artisans, merchants and grocers settled here.

This is reflected in the many different architectural styles around the Old Town Square. When in 1230 the district was given municipal rights by Wenceslas I, the prevailing style was Romanesque. Gothic came later. Given that the district was prone to flooding, many residents wisely decided to build upwards – in Baroque style. This is particularly apparent in *Husova* and *Celetná*. Many of the wine bars and restaurants that now occupy cellars there were originally at ground floor level.

Major changes also took place in the ● *Jewish Quarter* north of the Old Town Square. During the 13th century Prague's Jews were forced to move to a clearly-defined area on the right bank of the Vltava, known later as Josefov. They built their own schools, synagogues and houses there and the settlement grew rapidly. Its inhabitants, however, were often the victims of pogroms. More than 3,000 Jews died in the worst of these attacks during the Easter of 1389. Under Emperor Rudolf II (1576–1612), the neighbourhood prospered, as the tolerant ruler developed close contacts with members of the Jewish community. He even appointed Mordechai Maisel as his finance minister, but there were ulterior motives: the Jewish banker lent the art-obsessed emperor substantial sums of money so that he could extend his collections.

In 1848 the Jews were granted full civil rights, which meant among other things that they were now allowed to live outside Josefov. To some extent this meant a death sentence for the quarter. When the wealthy families moved out, the ghetto rapidly fell into disrepair. Towards the end of the 19th century, the city's administration decided to carry out a full-scale clearance of the Jewish quarter and to create a modern city in Parisian style. All the old houses were demolished and replaced. The showpiece in the revamped district was the elegant *Pařížská* boulevard, with its now highly-desirable Art Nouveau houses. Only a few buildings, the old cemetery, the town hall and six synagogues survived the clearance of old Josefov. During the World War II, the social fabric of the community was destroyed by the German occupiers and most of the inhabitants were murdered. Only the buildings were spared, because the Nazis wanted to create in Prague a 'Museum of the Extinct Race'.

In 1950 the so-called *Jewish Museum* came under state management. Only when communist regime fell was the Jewish community finally able to take charge of its own heritage. The museum's exhibitions are located at several sites, most of them in historic buildings in Josefov, including the main synagogues (see below). *Jewish Museum (Židovské muzeum) | April–Oct Sun–Fri 9am–6pm, Nov–March 9am–4.30pm | closed on Jewish holidays | 480Kč (all synagogues and the Old Cemetery) | www.jewishmuseum.cz*

■ CONVENT OF ST AGNES (ANEŽSKÝ KLÁŠTER) (128 C3) (*ⓜ G3*)

The early Gothic St Agnes Convent is in fact a complex containing two buildings – the Convent of the Poor Clares and the nearby Franciscan Minorite Monastery. Now it is home to a collection of medieval art from Bohemia and central Europe. Of particular interest in the convent's galleries are the bible-based pieces by Mas-

ter Theodoric, Bohemia's main Gothic painter, paintings by Lucas Cranach the Elder, the court painter to the Elector of Saxony, and also by Albrecht Altdorfer, a key figure in the Danube School. Sometimes described as the 'Bohemia's Assisi', the convent was founded in 1233 by King Wenceslas I, who is also buried here. The first abbess was his sister, later canonised as St Agnes of Bohemia. *Tue–Sun 10am–6pm | 150Kč | U Milosrdných 17 | www.ngprague.cz | metro: Staroměstská (A)*

■ OLD JEWISH CEMETERY (STARÝ ŽIDOVSKÝ HŘBITOV) ★ (128 B4) (*ⓜ F3*)

What appears to have been laid out for artistic effect actually emerged from a sheer lack of space. Under Jewish law graves must not be destroyed or tombstones removed, not even after a respectable time has elapsed. The solution was to simply add new soil. As a result, there are in some places as many as nine layers of graves on top of one other, and

Some 12,000 gravestones in the Old Jewish cemetery

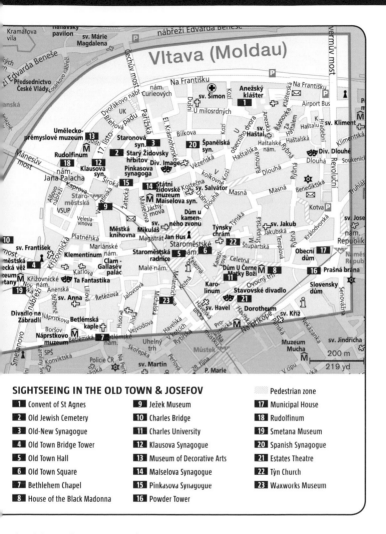

SIGHTSEEING IN THE OLD TOWN & JOSEFOV

▓▓▓ Pedestrian zone

1 Convent of St Agnes
2 Old Jewish Cemetery
3 Old-New Synagogue
4 Old Town Bridge Tower
5 Old Town Hall
6 Old Town Square
7 Bethlehem Chapel
8 House of the Black Madonna
9 Ježek Museum
10 Charles Bridge
11 Charles University
12 Klausova Synagogue
13 Museum of Decorative Arts
14 Malselova Synagogue
15 Pinkasova Synagogue
16 Powder Tower
17 Municipal House
18 Rudolfinum
19 Smetana Museum
20 Spanish Synagogue
21 Estates Theatre
22 Týn Church
23 Waxworks Museum

the elaborate headstones are heaped together randomly. The most famous grave in the cemetery is that of the creator of the legendary 'golem', Judah Liwa ben Bezallel, otherwise known as Rabbi Löw, who died in 1609. Records show that last burial took place here in May 1787, but when the first of an estimated 200,000 interments took place, no one really knows. The oldest of the 12,000 stones dates from 1439. By the way, if you are looking for the grave of Franz Kafka, it is not here – the celebrated writer is buried in the New Jewish Cemetery. *Široká 3 | opening times and admission: see Jewish Museum, p. 40 | metro: Staroměstská (A)*

THE OLD TOWN & JOSEFOV

▪3 OLD-NEW SYNAGOGUE (STARONOVÁ SYNAGOGA) ★

(128 B4) (*Ⓜ F3*)

The Old-New Synagogue was built around 1275 and is the oldest Gothic synagogue in Europe. One striking feature in the double-nave hall is the precision masonry, notably the delicate ornamentation on the *entrance portal*. According to legend, after it had been destroyed, angels brought a part of Solomon's temple to Prague from Jerusalem. And Rabbi Löw's clay golem also found its way here. It is said that its lifeless remains are lying in the synagogue's attic. The huge *flag* in the vault was presented to the Jews by Emperor Ferdinand II for their help in the valiant struggle against the Swedes in 1648. *Červená 2 | Sun–Thu April–Oct 9.30am–6pm, Nov–March 9.30am–5pm, Fri often only until 3pm | admission to Jewish Museum see p. 42 | metro: Staroměstská (A)*

navigation for see p.42

▪4 OLD TOWN BRIDGE TOWER (STAROMĚSTSKÁ MOSTECKÁ VĚŽ)

(128 A4) (*Ⓜ F4*)

Where today tourists from all over the world roam freely, in 1648 an army comprising mainly students and Jews repulsed an invading Swedish army, a victory that proved to be a decisive turning point in the Thirty Years' War. During the battle the ornamentation on the bridge side of the tower was destroyed. But this sturdy structure built to plans by Peter Parler around 1391 is still regarded as Europe's finest medieval bridge tower. The coats-of-arms above the gateway symbolise the ten lands that Charles IV brought together to form the Bohemian Kingdom. Next to them is a 'Kingfisher in a Love Knot', the symbol for Wenceslas IV, under whose reign the work on the tower was completed. Scratched on the walls in the dungeon are the remains of graffiti left by captives. *April–Sept daily 10am–*

10pm, March/Oct 10am–8pm, Nov–Feb 10am–6pm| 70Kč | Karlův most | metro: Staroměstská (A)

▪5 OLD TOWN HALL (STAROMĚSTSKÁ RADNICE) (128 B4) (*Ⓜ G4*)

Welcome to the 'most photographed group of men since the Beatles'. At least, that is what a Prague newspaper once called the twelve *apostles*, who emerge on the hour from two plain hatches in the town hall's tower. At peak times, hundreds of people gather in front of the south side of this early Gothic building to watch the spectacle. While on the subject of time, apart from the occasional malfunction, ever since 1410 the filigree *Astronomical Clock* has shown whether the stars are aligned. Perched on pinnacles are what were at the time perceived to be the 'four greatest threats to man-

kind': death with his hourglass, vanity admiring his reflection in a mirror, a Turk threatening more wars and a miser shaking a bulging bag.

In September 1338 King John of Luxembourg gave his consent for the construction of a town hall in the Staré Město, with the money coming from the proceeds of a wine tax. A few weeks later, the town council bought Wolflin the merchant's house and then after 1360 enlarged it. Neighbouring buildings were skilfully incorporated before the slender ☼ *tower* was raised as a 'symbol of secular power'. If you stand in the middle of the square and look up at the 70-m (230-ft) high structure, you will see quite clearly that at one time another town hall building was attached to it: the north wing was blown up by the Nazis in 1945, the day before the Soviet army marched

into Prague. The damaged facade with incomplete window frames has been left as a memorial. *Tue–Sun 9am–6pm, Mon 11am–8pm, tower: Mon 11am–10pm, Tue–Sun 9am–10pm | 100Kč | Tourist Information Centre | Staroměstské náměstí | metro: Staroměstská (A)*

■6 OLD TOWN SQUARE (STAROMĚSTSKÉ NÁMĚSTÍ) ★

(128 B4) (*M* G4)

Goods were traded on Prague's oldest square as long ago as the 12th century. In those days it was called the Great Square; this was where spices and vegetables, jewellery and silk, timber and cattle were exchanged. Before then, merchants used to meet in the courtyard behind the Týn Church, but had to pay a tax, known as an 'ungelt'. And that is what this square, opened in 1996 after

Top tourist attractions – the Old Town Square with the Old Town Hall and Týn Church

costly renovation work, is called today. Everything is still bought and sold on the Old Town Square. However, when it comes to what today's tourists are offered, quality and authenticity are no longer essential requirements.

In 1621 a dramatic historic event took place in the Old Town Square: after the Bohemian Estates lost the Battle of White Mountain, the victorious Catholic Habsburgs executed 27 Protestant

View from Town Hall Tower over the Old Town Square

nobles and lords here. Crosses cut into the pavement in front of the town hall remember the martyrs.

Jan Hus, whose *statue* stands in the middle of the square, also died a martyr. The work by sculptor Ladislav Šaloun shows the oppressed (left) and the defiant (right) at the feet of the reformer, who was burnt at the stake for heresy in Constance in 1415. At some time in their lives, celebrated residents of Prague, such as Franz Kafka, Albert Einstein and Bedřich

Smetana lived in the numerous Rococo, Renaissance and Gothic palaces around the square (look out for the plaques). *Metro: Staroměstská (A)*

7 BETHLEHEM CHAPEL (BETLEMSKÉ KAPLE) (128 B5) (*ɱ F4*)

The focal point inside this simple Gothic church is not the altar but the pulpit. Because this was where from 1402 to 1412 Jan Hus, the famous reformer, who was burned at the stake for heresy in Constance in 1415, addressed his congregation. His sermons, which he proclaimed in Czech, not in Latin, are said to have attracted up to 3000 people. Demolished during the 18th century, it was rebuilt in the 1950s using old drawings. *April–Oct daily 10am–6.30pm, Nov–March daily 10am–5.30pm | 50Kč | Betlemské náměstí 4 | metro: Staroměstská (A)*

8 HOUSE OF THE BLACK MADONNA (U ČERNÉ MATKY BOŽÍ) (128 C4) (*ɱ G4*)

The first Cubist residential house in Europe, built in 1911 to plans by Josef Gočár, houses a permanent exhibition of Czech Cubism, with furniture, paintings and architectural designs dating from between 1911 and 1919. Its name derives from the Baroque *Madonna figure* set in a niche on a corner of the facade. *Tue–Sun 10am–6pm | 100Kč | Ovocný trh 19 | metro: Náměstí Republiky (B)*

9 INSIDER TIP JEŽEK MUSEUM (PAMÁTNÍK JAROSLAVA JEŽKA) (128 B4) (*ɱ F4*)

The former home of composer Jaroslav Ježek (1906–42) is Prague's only *Jazz Museum* and also the smallest museum in the Czech capital. Covering an area of only 15sq m (160sq ft), a grand piano, desk and a variety of everyday items recall a musician who is highly regarded in the Czech Republic. The key to the 'Blue Room', as the museum is sometimes called, is kept by a music student who lives nearby. This alternative name for the museum has nothing to do with the blues or jazz. Ježek's eyesight was very poor and he found that the colour blue had a soothing effect. *Only Tue 1pm–6pm | 10Kč | Kaprova 10 | metro: Staroměstská (A)*

🔟 CHARLES BRIDGE (KARLŮV MOST)
★ ● ♒ (128 A4) *(🛏 F4)*

The 10-m (32-ft) wide and 520-m (1,700-ft) long bridge is a favourite haunt of Ukrainian caricature artists, Czech puppeteers and American guitarists, all vying for the attention of passers-by. For 400 years, the Gothic Charles Bridge resting on its 16 piers, was the only connection between the Old Town and the Lesser Town. Emperor Charles IV had it built in 1357 under the direction of Peter Parler, but under the original plans it was to remain unadorned. Most of the *statues* were added between 1657 and 1714, and it's hard to imagine the bridge without them today. The most famous figure has to be that of *St John of Nepomuk* (from the Old Town side the eighth figure on the right and, dating from 1683, one of the first to be erected). Revered as the patron saint of bridges, not just here, but in Bohemia, in Silesia, along the River Elbe and in Bavaria, he also protects the crews of river-going vessels against flooding and accidents. The bronze reliefs on the base are said to bring good luck if touched, and the smoothly polished surface indicates just how many people believe this to be the case. Between the sixth and seventh pillar on the right a *cross* on the parapet marks the place where 600 years ago John of Nepomuk was thrown into the river by King Wenceslas IV's henchmen. Despite being cruelly tortured, he refused to divulge the queen's confessional secrets. The first group of figures on the Charles Bridge depicts the *crucifixion scene* (1657, third statue on the right), the most recent the two canonised brothers from the 9th century, *Cyril and Methodius* (1938, fifth statue on the right).

In 2008, the bridge, by now over 650 years old, underwent comprehensive restoration work. This confirmed an an-

SIGHTSEEING WITH A DIFFERENCE

A bit of rain won't spoil your trip or cost you a lot of money – getting around by tram is cheap and convenient. For only 32Kč you can take tram no. 17 from the *Podolská vodárna* stop by the banks of the Vltava, pass the *Vyšehrad*, the Dancing House, the National Theatre, the Charles Bridge and the Rudolfinum as far as the *Výstaviště* exhibition grounds. There are even more sights to see on both sides of the *tramvaj* hub if you board the ● no. 22.

If you get on at *Náměstí Míru* direction *Bílá hora*, you will cross the New Town, pass the National Theatre, cross the Vltava to the Lesser Town and then after climbing to Hradčany continue as far as the Strahov Monastery *(Pohořelec)*. If you miss the stop, the tram carries on as far as the Břevnov Monastery *(Břevnovský klášter)* or the terminus at *Bílá hora*. But beware. The no. 22 is popularly known as the 'pickpocket express' – and for good reason!

cient legend: eggs had been added to the mortar. Be that has it may, the restoration was dogged with controversy with claims the contractors used the wrong kind of mortar and replaced too many of the old stones. Work was completed in 2011. *Old Town Bridge Tower see p. 44, Lesser Town Bridge Tower April–Sept daily 10am–10pm, March/Oct until 8pm, Nov–Feb until 6pm| 70Kč | metro: Malostranská (A)*

11 CHARLES UNIVERSITY (UNIVERZITA KARLOVA) (128 C4) (*G4*)

Even now, 650 years after it was founded, the name of this centre of learning still has a prestigious ring to it. Charles IV established the university on 7 April 1348. It was the first university in central Europe. The students had no campus to speak of. Lectures for the four faculties were held in monasteries and churches – at that time they were the only buildings suitable for large gatherings. It was 1383 before Wenc-

eslas IV donated to the Collegium Carolinum the Gothic house belonging to the former master of the mint, Johlin Rothlev. František M. Kanka was responsible for 'baroquising' the facade in 1718; at a later date the imposing *Great Hall* on the first floor underwent a major transformation. The *tapestry* there entitled 'Charles IV kneels before St Wenceslas' is by Václav Sychra (1947). Interestingly, the drapes with the coats-of-arms of the Bohemian lands have more than just a visual function: they were installed to improve the acoustics. The variegated stones on the facade of the Carolinum were added during the various renovation phases. They are intended to differentiate the old from the new. *Ovocný trh 5 | metro: Můstek (A, B)*

12 KLAUSOVA SYNAGOGUE (KLAUSOVA SYNAGOGA) (128 B4) (*F3*)

This Baroque building dating from the 17th century and situated near the old

SLAVIA OR SPARTA?

It could be football, it could be hockey – the local derby always pits Slavia against Sparta. Only a few die-hard fans gather in the football stadiums, but an Extraliga ice hockey game is a different matter, because ● *Lední hokej* is the national sport. Tickets are available from approx. 200Kč either on match day at the stadium or in advance.

▶ *HC Slavia Praha: O2 Arena | Ocelářské ulici 460/2 (*O1*) | www.hc-slavia.cz | metro: Českomoravská (B) | advance tickets sold at all Sazka booths*

▶ *HC Slavia Praha: Tesla Arena | Za-Elektrarnou 419 (*H1*) | www.hcsparta.cz |*

metro: Nádraží Holešovice(C) | advance tickets via Ticketportal

In football, AC Sparta is the Czech Republic's equivalent of Chelsea. Archrivals SK Slavia are perennial losers, but in 2008 and 2009 the underdogs won the championship in their new stadium. Tickets from 200Kč.

▶ *AC Sparta: Generali Arena | Milady Horákové 98 (127 E2) (*F2*) | www.sparta.cz | tram 1, 8, 25, 26: Sparta*

▶ *SK Slavia: Synot Tip Aréna | Vladivostocká 10 (*M7*) | www.slavia.cz | tram 6, 7, 22, 24: Slavia*

The Charles University is the oldest university in central Europe

Jewish cemetery houses a permanent exhibition illustrating Jewish traditions, everyday items, customs and holidays. Key exhibits include some rare Hebrew prints. *U starého hřbitova 1 | opening/ admission: see Jewish Museum, p. 42 | metro: Staroměstská (A)*

13 MUSEUM OF DECORATIVE ARTS (UMĚLECKOPRŮMYSLOVÉ MUZEUM)
(128 B4) (*Ø F3*)

On show here is the largest glass collection in the world. Prepare to feast your eyes on no fewer than 16,000 exhibits in glass, porcelain and ceramics; other sections cover clocks, watches, measuring instruments, Cubist furniture and lots more. Reliefs on the building's facade represent the various crafts. *Wed–Sun 10am–6pm, Tue 10am–7pm | 120Kč | Ulice 17. listopadu 2 | metro: Staroměstská (A)*

14 MAISELOVA SYNAGOGUE (MAISELOVA SYNAGOGA)
(128 B4) (*Ø F3*)

Once the largest synagogue in Prague, it was commissioned by Mordechai Maisel at the end of the 16th century. After a fire in 1689 it was reduced in size and then at the beginning of the 19th century it was converted into neo-Gothic style. Silver treasure from many Bohemian synagogues is kept here. *Maiselova 10 | admission and opening times: see Jewish Museum p. 42 | metro: Staroměstská (A)*

15 PINKASOVA SYNAGOGUE (PINKASOVA SYNAGOGA)
(128 B4) (*Ø F3*)

Prague's most ornate synagogue was built in 1530 by Aaron Meshullam Horowitz. The late-Gothic building was extended in the 17th century, when a lobby and women's gallery was added. A chilling reminder of the holocaust can be seen on the walls of the synagogue. Listed here are the names of the 77,297 Jews from Bohemia and Moravia who were killed between 1939 and 1945. Diaries, letters, poems and drawings document the horrors endured by some of the victims of Terezín concentration camp. *Široká 3 | opening times/admission: see Jewish Museum p. 42 | metro: Staroměstská (A)*

16 POWDER TOWER (PRAŠNÁ BRÁNA) ☼ (128 C4) (*꧁ G4*)

The length of time it took to complete this building must be a record! Work on the Gothic tower started in 1475, but it was not completed for another 400 years. In 1484 they broke off the work on the ceremonial structure because the then ruler, King Vladislav, moved his court from the Old Town to the castle. The 65-m (210-ft) high tower was given a temporary roof and at the end of the 17th century it was used to store gunpowder (hence the name). A hipped roof was added during restoration work in 1886. *April–Sept 10am–10pm, March/Oct 10am–8pm, Nov–Feb 10am–6pm | 70Kč | Celetná | metro: Náměstí Republiky (B)*

17 MUNICIPAL HOUSE (OBECNÍ DŮM) (128 C4) (*꧁ G4*)

This stunning example of Czech Art Nouveau architecture would probably never have happened if King Vladislav had not moved his residence. Built on the ruins of the old royal court is the imposing Municipal House (1906–11) with Karel Špillar's semi-circular mosaic entitled ‹Homage to Prague› above the main entrance.

Every year, the Prague Spring Festival, a prestigious music event, is held in the *Smetana Concert Hall*, easily the Municipal House's high spot. Also located in the *Repre,* as the Municipal House is often described in local parlance, are five more rooms, two restaurants and a café. The renovation of the *Obecní dům* (which translated into English means 'community centre') during the 1990s cost about 60 million euros.

Guided tours take place several times a day *(280Kč)*. For more information ask at the desk on the ground floor or call *2 22 00 21 01. Náměstí Republiky 5 | metro: Náměstí Republiky (B)*

18 RUDOLFINUM (128 B4) (*꧁ F3*)

The Municipal House has the Smetana Hall, whereas the Rudolfinum (1876–84) honours the Czech Republic's second musical genius. In the *House of Artists* (as this neo-Renaissance building is also officially known) an impressive colonnade leads to the *Dvořák Concert Hall*. The design by architects Josef Schulz and Josef Zítek also included a grand *flight of steps*, which is often used as the backdrop for TV commercials. The building, which was named not after Emperor Rudolf but the project's patron Crown Prince Rudolf, was officially opened by Antonín Dvořák. And he it was who conducted the first concert in the hall that bears his name in 1896. For a short time (1919–39), the building was home to the Czechoslovak parliament. Interesting temporary exhibitions are held in the gallery and it is also used for cultural events. *Tue–Sun 10am–6pm (Thu until 8pm) | Alšovo nábřeží 12 | 140Kč | www.galerierudolfinum.cz | metro: Staroměstská (A)*

19 SMETANA MUSEUM (MUZEUM BEDŘICHA SMETANY) (128 A5) (*꧁ F4*)

There could be no better spot for a memorial to Bedřich Smetana (1824–84), the composer of the famous ‹Vltava› movement from the ‹Má vlast› symphonic cycle. Located by the banks of the river, the museum keeps original manuscripts and correspondence by the principal exponent of Czech national music. Also on display here is Smetana's piano, now renovated several times, plus numerous costumes from his operas (e.g. ‹The Bartered Bride'). The six-part ‹Má vlast› was completed around 1874 and premièred in 1882, by which time Smetana was already almost completely deaf. *Wed–Mon 10am–5pm | 50Kč | Novotného lávka 1 | metro: Staroměstská (A)*

20 SPANISH SYNAGOGUE (ŠPANĚLSKÁ SYNAGOGA) (128 B3) (*G3*)

The newest synagogue in Josefov dates from 1868. Its name is derived from its Moorish style, not because it was used at any time by Spanish or Sephardic Jews. After extensive renovation work, with practically every surface covered by richly ornamented, Islamic-style polychrome and gilded patterns, it has been open to visitors for some years now. An exhibition documents the story behind the Jewish community in the Czech Republic. *Vězeňská 1 | opening/admission: see Jewish Museum, p. 42 | metro: Staroměstská (A)*

21 ESTATES THEATRE (STAVOVSKÉ DIVADLO) (128 C4) (*G4*)

This neoclassical building, commissioned by Count Franz Anton Nostitz Rieneck, was built in 1781–3 to a design by Anton Haffenecker. Originally called the Nostitz Theatre, the first performance was 'Emilia Galotti', by the German dramatist, Gotthold Ephraim Lessing. The first performance in the Czech language took place in 1785, before Mozart conducted his 'Don Giovanni' here on 29 October 1787. At that time the theatre had not yet adopted its present name. The Bohemian Estates did not take it over until 1799. From 1945 until 1991 it was called the Tyl Theatre after the co-author of the national anthem, Josef Kajetán Tyl (1808–56). His composition entitled 'Kde domov můj?'('Where is my homeland?') was given its first performance here. *Ovocný trh 1 | metro: Můstek (A, B)*

22 TÝN CHURCH (MATKA BOŽÍ PŘED TÝNEM) (128 C4) (*G4*)

This masterpiece of Bohemian Gothic (1365–1511) with its ⚜ 80-m (260-ft) high towers dominates the Old Town Square. The sturdier right-hand tower (called 'Adam') gives the slimmer 'Eve'

The Spanish Synagogue in Moorish-style

some shade during the summer, thus helping to lower the internal temperature – that was important at a time when 'Eve' was used as a warehouse for storing perishable goods. The *Madonna statue* was not added to the facade until the 17th century. Adorning the high stone

cause of death. That was inconclusive, so in 2010 samples of bone, hair and clothing were analysed. Was he murdered? Did he die of poisoning or a disease? Despite all the analyses, his death remains a mystery. *Services Sun 9.30am, 9pm, Sat 8am, Sept–June Tue–Thu 6pm,*

A golden madonna adorns a gable high above the portal of the Týn Church

gable before then was a huge chalice, an emblem of the Hussites, who celebrated the Eucharist with bread and wine. After their defeat in 1620, the chalice was melted down and used to make a halo, sceptre and crown for the Virgin Mary. Near to the main altar in the rather plain interior of the church is the *gravestone* of Tycho Brahe (1546–1601). The Danish astronomer to Emperor Rudolf II wore a nose made of gold and silver, because he had lost his own in a duel. In 2010 Brahe was buried in the Týn church for the third time. An autopsy was performed on his body in 1901 to see if they could find a

Fri 3pm, Sat 8am, July/Aug Mon–Fri 12.15pm; tours Tue–Sat 10am–1pm, 3pm–5pm, Sun 10.30am–noon | Staroměstské náměstí | metro: Staroměstská (A)

23 WAXWORKS MUSEUM (MUZEUM VOSKOVÝCH FIGURÍN)
(128 C5) (*M* G4)

Franz Kafka, Fidel Castro, Karel Gott – a total of 50 famous, in some cases, infamous personalities from Czech history, but also of international renown, are exhibited in four rooms here. *Daily 9am–8pm | 150Kč | Melantrichova 5 | metro: Můstek (A, B)*

NEW TOWN/ NOVÉ MĚSTO

The creation of this quarter of the city was one of the largest town-planning projects ever undertaken in the Middle Ages – and like so much in Prague, it is attributable to the German Emperor and the Bohemian king, Charles IV. He wanted to expand Prague and make it into the capital of his empire. One of the most important elements in his plan was the establishment of a completely new district. So in 1348 he had a wall built around the Old Town enclosing an area of approx. 500 acres – that marked the birth of the new town. Charles IV was also concerned with the details. He set the height of the houses and specified the street lay-out. The roads had to be up to 25m (80ft) wide so that 'at least two teams of horses could pass each other'. He also decreed that tradesmen who 'cause noise and dirt', such as tanners, carpenters and black-smiths, would have to move from the Old Town into the New Town. At the centre of it there were to be three large squares: the cattle market *(Karlovo náměstí)*, the hay market *(Senovažné náměstí)* and the horse market, which was later renamed Wenceslas Square *(Václavské náměstí)* and is now probably the city's most famous landmark. It's true – there are much nicer places in Prague than *Václavák*, as the locals call it. Rather tired and scruffy, it is a long way from being a prestigious, Paris-style boulevard – and yet Wenceslas Square is to this day the place where the nation congregates at decisive moments in its history. When in 1968 Warsaw Pact troops brutally crushed the Prague Spring, the harrowing pictures of events taking place on Wenceslas Square were beamed around the world.

During the 1980s, on the instructions of Minister of the Interior, Lubomir Strougal, a green strip was painted in the middle of the square to prevent demonstrations. A few years later the square was once again the focal point for protests against the communist regime. When in November 1989 Vaclav Havel addressed the thousands of demonstrators from the balcony of the Melantrich Publishing House, nothing was going to stop the movement for democratic change.

The New Town is nowhere near as picturesque as the Old Town or the Lesser Town, but it is nevertheless a lively spot. An ancient ditch that marked the boundary between the Old Town and the New Town is now Prague's main shopping area *(Na příkopě)*. Numerous museums, theatres and music clubs are located in the New Town. If you are interested in architecture, there is plenty to see. Examples of Cubism (below the Vysehrad) and contemporary design (Frank O. Gehry's Dancing House) can be viewed here, as can some grand 19th century buildings, such as the National Museum and the National Theatre.

◼1 BEER MUSEUM (PIVOVARSKÉ MUZEUM) ● (131 E2) (ⓜ F5)

The story of beer and brewing is attractively documented in the former malt house for U Fleků, a famous Prague restaurant. Expert guides are on hand to explain the functions of the various exhibits. *Mon–Fri 10am–4pm, Sat/Sun only for restaurant guests | 50Kč, tour of the brewery 160Kč | please book in advance on 2 24 93 40 19 | Křemencova 11 | metro: Národní třída (B)*

◼2 DVOŘÁK MUSEUM (MUZEUM ANTONÍNA DVOŘÁKA) (132 B3) (ⓜ G6)

This museum, dedicated to the celebrated Czech composer, Antonín Dvořák

(1841–1904), is worth a visit for its architectural interest alone. Built to a design by Kilian Ignaz Dientzenhofer for Count Michna, the Baroque summer palace dates from 1712. It was Dientzenhofer's first building in Prague. Some say the name Villa America is derived from a former inn nearby, but it is an appropriate title as it fits with Dvořák's life story. After all, he lived for several years in New York, where he was artistic director at the Conservatory from 1892 to 1895 and it is also where he composed the 'New World' symphony. There is a reconstruction of his study in the museum. *April–Sept Tue, Wed, Fri–Sun 10am–1.30pm, 2pm–5.30pm, Thu 11am–3.30pm, 4pm–7pm, Oct–March Tue–Sun 10am–1.30pm, 2pm–5pm | 50Kč | Ke Karlovu 20 | metro: I. P. Pavlova (C)*

The Dvořák Museum is housed in a Baroque palace

3 INSIDER TIP FRANCISCAN GARDEN (FRANTIŠKÁNSKÁ ZAHRADA) ● (128 C5) (*ω G5*)

This island of tranquillity surrounded by brick and concrete with numerous benches and footpaths is close to busy Wenceslas Square – access from the square through the Světozor Passage. The site of the garden was once a place of eternal rest – part of it was built on a former cemetery belonging to the Franciscan Order. *Jungmannovo náměstí | metro: Můstek (A, B)*

4 CHURCH OF OUR LADY OF THE SNOWS (KOSTEL PANNY MARIE SNĚŽNÉ) (128 C5) (*ω G4*)

Charles IV also commissioned churches. One of them was the Church of Our Lady of the Snows, work on which began in 1347. It was the emperor's wish that it should be used as the coronation church. So the original plans were of ambitious proportions; he wanted it to be bigger and better than the St Vitus Cathedral. Work on it was interrupted by the Hussite Wars, and in the 17th century a conversion to Renaissance style was started. With a nave height of 33m (110ft), Our Lady of the Snows is the tallest Gothic church in the capital. Above Prague's largest altar stands Václav Vavřinec Reiner's painting 'The Annunciation' of 1724. *Daily 7am–7pm | Jungmannovo náměstí | metro: Můstek (A, B)*

5 MUSEUM OF COMMUNISM (MUZEUM KOMUNISMU) (127 F5) (*ω G4*)

Before the Velvet Revolution, the Sylva Taroucca Palace was the home of the Socialist Education Association. Since 2001, this Baroque edifice designed by Kilian Ignaz Dientzenhofer around 1740 has been exhibiting assorted memorabilia ranging from busts of Lenin to posters for the Czechoslovakian May Day parade

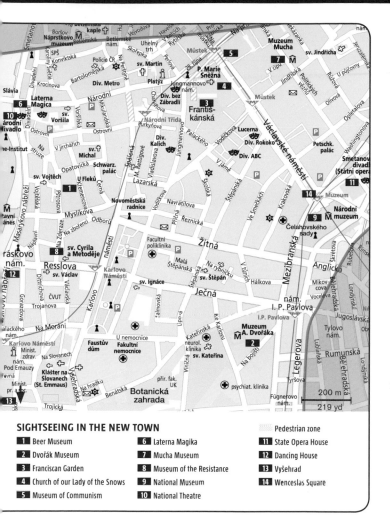

SIGHTSEEING IN THE NEW TOWN

1 Beer Museum
2 Dvořák Museum
3 Franciscan Garden
4 Church of our Lady of the Snows
5 Museum of Communism
6 Laterna Magika
7 Mucha Museum
8 Museum of the Resistance
9 National Museum
10 National Theatre
11 State Opera House
12 Dancing House
13 Vyšehrad
14 Wenceslas Square
Pedestrian zone

in the period between 1948 and 1989. The driving force behind the museum was the American Glenn Spicker. This and a similar museum in Latvia are the only communist museums in the former Eastern bloc. *Daily 9am–9pm | 180Kč | Na příkopě 10 | www.muzeumkomunismu.cz | metro: Můstek (A, B)*

6 LATERNA MAGIKA (128 B5) (*Ø F5*)
For decades a dispute raged about what should fill the gap next to the grandiose National Theatre. It was 1977 before work began on the construction of the glass facade following a bold design by Karel Prager. The interior of the building is adorned with green marble slabs

The Louvre was the prototype for the National Museum

from Cuba. Its rather plain auditorium is shaped like an amphitheatre. When it was completed in 1983, the theatre was named the *Nová scená* (New Stage). Only later did the Laterna Magika move here from the basement of the Palais Adria. In its performances, the pantomime effects of classic black light theatre are complemented by video technology. *Nova scéna | Narodni Trida 4 | tel. 2 24 93 14 82 | www.laterna.cz | metro: Narodni Trida (B)*

7 MUCHA MUSEUM (128 C5) (*M G4*)

This museum showcases the work of the versatile Art Nouveau artist Alfons Mucha (1860–1939). Although some of his photographic work is on show, a lot of the pieces here are graphics (e.g. posters for the French actress, Sarah Bernhardt) and paintings depicting scenes from Slavic history. *Daily 10am–6pm | 180Kč | Panská 7 | www.mucha.cz | metro: Můstek (A, B)*

8 INSIDER TIP MUSEUM OF THE RESISTANCE (PAMÁTNÍK HRDINŮ) (131 E3) (*M F6*)

After the assassination of Obergruppenführer Reinhard Heydrich, the Acting Reich Protector of Bohemia and Moravia, in June 1942, his assailants fought a heroic battle against the overwhelming forces of the Waffen SS at the Orthodox Cathedral of Saints Cyril and Methodius. This rather sparse exhibition retells the tragic events of that day, when the last resistance fighters, who had taken refuge in the crypt, chose to take their own lives rather than surrender. Outside, bullet holes can still be seen around the opening above the crypt and there is a commemorative plaque. *March–Oct Tue–Sun 9am–5pm, Nov–Feb Tue–Sat 9am–5pm | 75Kč | Resslova 9 | metro: Karlovo náměstí (B)*

9 NATIONAL MUSEUM (NÁRODNÍ MUZEUM) (132 B2) (*M H5*)

It's all stirring stuff celebrating Czech nationhood – in the wings there are extensive ethnographic, archaeological and natural science collections, including the largest *collection of minerals* in Europe. Other prized exhibits include the *library* (with over 3.5 million volumes) and the *coin collection*. In a two-storey pantheon at the heart of museum, built around 1890, are some 50 or so bronze statues of distinguished Czechs. The neo-Renaissance facade is based on the Louvre in Paris. A major restoration process is underway and the historic building will be closed until probably June 2015.

Also part of the National Museum is the adjoining complex of buildings, which was extended in the 1960s *(Vinohradská 1)*. Originally the stock market, then – during the communist era – the seat of the parliament and finally the studios of Radio Free Europe, it has witnessed many changes in Czech society. The National Museum now stages temporary exhibitions here. *Daily 10am–6pm, every first Wed in the month until 8pm, closed every first Tue in the month | historic buildings 150Kč, new building 100Kč, combined ticket 200Kč | Václavské náměstí 68 | www.nm.cz | metro: Muzeum (A, C)*

🔟 NATIONAL THEATRE (NÁRODNÍ DIVADLO) (128 B5) (*ⓜ F5*)

This neo-Renaissance building dates from 1868 and stands on the site of Prague's salt warehouse. The country's Habsburg masters refused to fund the theatre, so a nationwide campaign to raise the money was organised and eventually it could be built, to a design by Josef Zítek. But shortly after it was opened (with a performance of Smetana's 'Libuse') on 12 August 1881 a fire reduced the theatre to ashes. The reconstruction was declared a national duty, and it took the Czechs barely six weeks to turn dream into reality. Before long work on the new building had started, this time under the direction of Josef Schulz, and on 18 November 1883 the theatre was officially re-opened. The nation's best artists contributed to the fittings – the amazing *curtain* above the stage was the work of Václav Hynais. *Národní třída 2 | tel. 2 24 90 14 82 | www.narodni-divadlo.cz | metro: Národní třída (B)*

🔢 STATE OPERA HOUSE (STÁTNÍ OPERA) (129 D6) (*ⓜ H5*)

Cut off from the city centre by the urban expressway, the neoclassical State Opera House stands between the Art Nouveau main railway station and the rather functional parliament building dating from the 1970s. Until 1885 a wooden 'New Town Theatre' occupied this space, but that was demolished and three years later, the 'German Theatre' opened with a performance of the Wagner's quintessentially German 'Die Meistersänger von Nürnberg'. The Viennese architects, Ferdinand Fellner and Herman Helmer, were responsible for its design.

It later changed its name to the 'New German Theatre' and in 1949 to the 'Smetana Theatre'. Since 1992 though, the richly ornamented building, where Richard Wagner's 'Ring des Nibelungen' was performed no fewer than 50 times between 1888 and 1938, has been known as the 'State Opera House'. Further evidence for the stage's German origins can be seen on the **INSIDER TIP** *facade*: beside the Dionysos chariot and Thalia, the muse of comedy, are portraits of the celebrated German dramatists, Goethe and Schiller. *Legerova 75 |* *tel. 2 24 22 72 66 | www.opera.cz | metro: Muzeum (A, C)*

12 INSIDER TIP DANCING HOUSE (TANČÍCÍ DŮM) ● **(131 D3)** *(Ø F6)*

The American architect, Frank O. Gehry, and his colleague, Vlado Milunic, came up with a bold design to fill the gap left in a row of houses caused by a World War II bomb. The residents of Prague love the building. Shortly after the topping-out ceremony, the bizarre, twisted structure acquired the nickname Ginger and Fred, after the Hollywood dancing duo of Ginger Rogers and Fred Astaire. Perched on the top of the building is a hemisphere made of perforated sheet metal. The curves painted on to the facade represent the waves of the Vltava River. Former Czech president Václav Havel owned the

RELAX & ENJOY

Noisy trams, traffic congestion and hordes of tourists – a gentle stroll through Prague can easily turn into a struggle. But it's not difficult to find peace and relaxation, especially in the Lesser Town. You will still find, amid all the commotion, some serene sanctuaries where you can pause and draw breath. *Zahrada* or garden is the magic word. Almost every grand mansion had its own, sometimes quite large, patch of greenery. What once was the preserve of the upper echelons of society is now in most cases open to all. The *Wallenstein Garden* **(126 C4)** *(Ø E3)* (*Valdštejnská zahrada, Letenská | April/ May/Oct daily 10am–6pm, June–Sept 10am–7pm*) is one of the largest. It belongs to a palace of the same name, where today the Senate, the Czech parliament's upper house, meets. Bronze statues, fountains, parading peacocks and an owl aviary make a great backdrop for a quiet interlude. A nondescript drive leads to another jewel of Baroque horticulture: *Vrtba Garden* **(126 C5)** *(Ø E4)* (*Vrtbovská zahrada, Karmelitská 25 | April–Oct daily 10am– 6pm | 58Kč*) and its outbuildings were used as a kindergarten during the communist era – and during that time they fell into a state of disrepair. They have since been smartened up and leisure gardeners will enjoy taking a stroll here. The *Vojan Garden* **(127 D4)** *(Ø E3)* (*U lužického semináře 17 | daily 8am– 5pm, in summer until 7pm*) is one of the city's oldest. Sit on a park bench in the shade of fruit trees and take a well-earned break.

detached house nextdoor (no. 78), having lived in it as a child. *Rašínovo nábřeží 80 | metro: Karlovo náměstí (B)*

⛶ VYŠEHRAD ★ (131 E5–6) (⍔ F7)

Only at the weekend are you likely to meet many walkers on the bizarre Vltava Rock; most visitors to Prague tend to avoid Vyšehrad. That is their loss, because they would appreciate the fine view over the city from the ⛨ Church of St Peter and Paul. It was from this hill that in around 725 Princess Libuše, matriarch of the Přemyslid dynasty, foresaw in Prague 'glory that reaches to the stars'. The Bohemian princes later founded a settlement here. Among the ruins of the first castle, most of which was destroyed in the 15th century during the Hussite Wars, is the Romanesque *St Martin's Rotunda*. Dating from the 12th century, it is one of Prague's oldest buildings. Nearby a gateway leads to an underground store, where many original statues from the Czech capital are protected from decay.

Pass through a portal next to the church facade and you will come to the ● *Cemetery of Honour*, the focal point here being the *Slavín monument*. Many distinguished personalities from Czech history are buried here, including the composers Bedřich Smetana and Antonín Dvořák, the conductor Rafael Kubelík, the artist Alfons Mucha and the writers Karel Čapek, Jan Neruda and Božena Němcová. The first cultural hero to be buried here in 1901 was the poet, Julius Zeyer. *Slavín monument Nov–Feb, daily 8am–5pm, March/April/Oct until 6pm, May–Sept until 7pm | Vyšehradské sady | metro: Vyšehrad (C)*

⛶ WENCESLAS SQUARE (VÁCLAVSKÉ NÁMĚSTÍ) ★
(128 C5–6) (⍔ G4–5)

A busy plaza for those in a hurry, for strollers, lovers, urban explorers, idlers

Doing the twist – Frank Gehry's Dancing House

A proud King Wenceslas surveys his square

... and pickpockets – that is Wenceslas Square today. It boasts two metro stations, ten bureaux de change, countless offices, shops and restaurants, and yet when Charles IV planned it in 1348, he saw it as a horse market outside the Old Town's gates. Some 500 years later, the Bohemian uprising against the Habsburgs started here. As an act of defiance, the nationalists named the 750-m long and 60-m wide square after the country's patron saint, *Wenceslas*. A *bronze statue* of the good king on horseback stands in front of the imposing National Museum at the upper end of the square. Standing guard beside him on a lower plinth are more patron saints, namely Agnes, Ludmila, Prokop and Adalbert. It was close to this monument that student Jan Palach set fire to himself on 16 Jan 1969 to protest against the lethargy of the people after the Warsaw Pact countries snuffed out the Prague Spring (INSIDERTIP memorial stone in embedded in the pavement outside the National Museum).

A major facelift for the square is currently in the pipeline. The aim is to widen pavements, reduce traffic to a minimum and also to cut the number of fast-food stands. In addition, a tramline will run through the square, just as it did in 1980.

IN OTHER QUARTERS

HOLEŠOVICE (129 E–F 1–2) (*ĎJ H–K1*)

This district in a bend in the Vltava is one of Prague's most popular residential quarters. And that is partly attributable to the two parks: *Stromovka Park (arboretum)* was originally created as a royal deer park. Now the area is often teeming with walkers, cyclists and inline skaters. On the Letná plateau, where today an oversized *metronom*e symbolically ticks back and forth, once stood the largest monument to Stalin in the Soviet bloc (128 B2) (*ΩΩ F2–3*). Blown up in 1962, what is left of the statue's ● granite pedestal is the place to stand if you want a ↘↗ superb panoramic view of Prague and the bridges over the Vltava.

But the district also has some cultural offerings: The *Lapidárium (Wed noon–4pm, Thu–Sun noon–6pm | 50Kč | Výstaviště 422* (0) *(ΩΩ H1)* | *tram 5, 12, 17: Výstaviště)* is, as it were, the National Museum's museum. The building, dating from 1891, houses sculptures that were either unfinished or damaged or likely to suffer weather damage (including some INSIDERTIP original statues from the Charles Bridge).

The ★ *Collection of Modern Art (Sbírka moderního umění)* is the Czech capital's finest art gallery *(Tue–Sun 10am–6pm | 250Kč | Dukelských hrdinů 47* (129 D1) *(ΩΩ H1)* | *www.ngprague.cz | tram 5, 12, 17: Veletržni)*. The centrepiece is undoubtedly the collection of pieces by 19th and 20th century masters, including 130 paintings and 50 sculptures by, among others, Paul Cézanne, Marc Chagall, Paul Gauguin, Vincent van Gogh and Pablo Picasso – a truly impressive compilation! Covering a vast area in the former Trade Fair Palace, the gallery also showcases important works by Czech artists.

Holešovice is also the site of Prague's largest modern art gallery, the INSIDERTIP *DOX Centre for Contemporary Art (Sat–Mon 10am–6pm, Wed–Fri 11am–7pm | 180Kč | Poupětova 1* (0) *(ΩΩ J–K1)* | *www. doxprague.org | tram 5, 12: Ortenovo Náměstí)*. DOX is a reference to the ancient Greek word for 'that which is thought to be true'. The rooms in this former factory stage temporary exhibitions from the world of the visual arts, architecture and design. There is also a café and design shop.

SMÍCHOV (130 A–C 5–6) *(ΩΩ C–E 7–8)*
Staropramen, Prague's largest brewery, welcomes beer enthusiasts to its *Visitor Centre (Pivovarská 9* (131 D5) *(ΩΩ E7)* | *Tue–Sat 10am–6pm, guided tours daily, 1pm in English | 199Kč | for bookings call 2 57 19 13 00 | metro: Anděl (B))*. Bohemian cuisine washed down with fresh *pivo* is served in the brewhouse café.

Smíchov is also home to the *Mozart Museum*, which occupies the *Villa Bertramka (daily 10am–11pm | 150Kč | Mozartova 169* (130 B4) *(ΩΩ D7)* | *metro: Anděl (B))*. Between 1787 and 1791 the young Mozart was often a guest at the villa and he wrote the overture for 'Don Giovanni' here.

VINOHRADY & ŽIŽKOV
(132–133 C–F 1–2) *(ΩΩ H–K 4–5)*
Vinohrady or 'vineyards' is blessed with many large, often finely renovated old buildings. As one of the city's most expensive residential quarters, it is much favoured by wealthy foreigners. It is worth making the trip to *Rieger Park (Riegerovy sady) (132–133 C–D2) (ΩΩ J5)*; the large beer garden here is one of its main attractions.

In the nearby district of Žižkov stands Prague's tallest structure, the *television tower (Televizní věž)*. From its 93-m (305-ft) ↘↗ high visitors' platform, the view extends in all directions *(Mahlerovy sady 1* (133 E2) *(ΩΩ K5)* | *daily 10am–10pm | 120Kč)*.

The same goes for ↘↗ *Vítkov Hill*, topped by a huge granite monument used by the communists as a mausoleum. Now an exhibition documents the history of Czechoslovakia. If you have had your fill of history lessons, go straight to the café on the roof terrace *(Wed–Sun 10am–6pm | 110Kč | U Památníku 1900* (129 F4) *(ΩΩ K4)* | *tram 1, 9, 16: Ohrada)*.

The renovation programme has been slow to reach this rather rundown, former working class district. Žižkov is the centre of Prague's alternative culture. There are some small theatres, *Akropolis*, a popular music club, plus countless bars. One important landmark for literature buffs is the INSIDER TIP *New Jewish Cemetery (Nový Židovský hřbitov)*, mainly because it is Franz Kafka's last resting place *(April–Sept Sun–Thu 9am–5pm, Fri 9am–2pm, Oct– March Sun–Thu 9am–4pm, Fri 9am–2pm | Izraelská 1 (0) (☐ N5) | metro: Želivského (A))*. The grave of the writer who died in 1924 is to be found in the first row of headstones, when coming from the 'Don Giovanni' hotel (third entrance). Also worth a look are the graves of soldiers from both world wars.

ŠÁRKA VALLEY (DIVOKÁ ŠÁRKA) (0) (☐ 0)

About 7km (4mi) as the crow flies west of the city centre lies the Šárka valley. It's hard to imagine that you are on the outskirts of a city with more than a million inhabitants. Steep-sided slate and sandstone rocks line the path through the nature reserve beside a stream known as the Šárka. The *open-air swimming pool (in summer daily 9am–7pm | 60Kč)* in a pretty clearing is fed by cool water from the stream. A little further on is a beer garden, which is very popular with cyclists during the summer. (Tram 20, 26: Divoká Šárka, then a ten-minute walk along the red-marked path)

OUTSIDE THE CITY

KARLŠTEJN CASTLE (134 C5) (☐ 0)

In 1348 on a rock surrounded by woodland 30km (19mi) southwest of Prague, Charles IV built an impregnable fortress – he needed somewhere safe for his

Karlštejn Castle – once an impregnable fortress, now a tourist attraction

valuable possessions. Stored here were royal treasures and the crown jewels of the Holy Roman Empire of the German nation. The imposing fortress site offers an amazing view of the surrounding countryside. *Nov– March Tue–Sun 10am–3pm, April/Oct Tue–Sun 10am–5pm, May/June/Sept Tue–Sun 10am–6pm, July/Aug Tue–Sun 10am–7pm | only as part of a guided tour (two versions) 270–300Kč | www.hradkarlstejn.cz / several trains daily, journey time approx. 40 min.*

PRŮHONICE (133 D4) *(Ⓜ 0)*

Many fairy tales have been filmed against the backdrop of Průhonice Castle. But don't make the trip to the village, which lies just beyond the Prague's southern boundary, just for the castle. Although the building dates from the 14th century, it has had many makeovers since then. The main attraction is the

huge park. In 2010 it became a Unesco World Heritage site.

The 23km (14mi) of walking trails are very popular and some 1,600 different plants grow here. In the spring it is a riot of blossom. The park is noted especially for its beautiful rhododendrons. It's a delightful spot, and not just for botanists! *Nov–Feb 8am–5pm, March 7am–6pm, April, Oct 7am–7pm, May–Sept 7am–8pm | 50Kč | from Opatov metro station (C) approx. 15 min, then onward with buses 363, 385 to the Průhonice stop*

TEREZÍN (134 C2) *(Ⓜ 0)*

During the 18th century the Habsburgs built this garrison town 50km (31mi) north of Prague as a bulwark against the Prussians. After the occupation of Bohemia and Moravia in World War II, the Nazis chose Terezín as the site of a a concentration camp. The 'little fortress' became a Gestapo prison and the town itself became a ghetto for tens of thousands of Jews. All the original inhabitants were evacuated. More than 30,000 people were murdered in Terezín, about 90,000 more were deported to extermination camps. The Ghetto Museum impressively documents the story of the camp and also details the appalling living conditions prisoners had to endure between 1941 and 1945. Today approximately 3,000 people live in Terezín. *Memorial in the Small Fortress: Nov–March daily 8am–4.30pm, April–Oct daily 8am–6pm | 160Kč | Principova alej 304 | www.pamatnik-terezin.cz*
Ghetto Museum in the town: Nov–March daily 9am–5.30pm | April–Oct daily 9am–6pm | 160Kč | Máchova 178
Every day several buses leave from Horenc bus station to Terezín. By train make for nearby Litoměřice. Journey time approx. 45 min.

FOOD & DRINK

There were times when Bohemian cuisine had a worldwide reputation. **In the days of the Austro-Hungarian Empire, wealthy families would appoint a chef from Bohemia. But that was a long time ago. Local cuisine has still not yet fully recovered from forty years of communism.** A few restaurants are gradually moving Bohemian cooking away from commercial sauces-in-a-bag and seasoning mixes. If you want to dine out in style the Bohemian way, then you will probably have to dig deep into your pockets and know where you have to go. When the communist regime fell, the people of Prague were eager to embrace new ideas. Pizzerias and fast food chains were the first to move in. Now, the range is huge and the quality high. It could be

sushi, tapas or bagels – specialities from all over the world are now commonplace and the standards are often higher than local cuisine. The citizens of Prague have also rediscovered the coffee house culture. There are now plenty of places to sit and read the newspaper, to drink cappuccino – the Louvre, the Imperial or the Slavia, for example. Friends meet up here for a chat, some just want to while away an afternoon with a good book. The locals don't seem too bothered by the presence of all the tourists, who are, of course, also drawn to the smart cafés. Who could forget, though, that Prague was and remains Europe's beer (pivo) capital? The word pivo comes from *pít*, meaning 'to drink'. It is the original wort (not to be confused with the alcohol con-

---

Photo: Old Town Square with the Týn Church in the background

For decades, Prague cuisine lacked creativity, but chefs have since found inspiration further afield

tent) that determines the flavour. A 10° beer is the norm and is similar to a continental lager, a 12° beer is bitter and more akin to a strong lager. But remember that these values are not the same as alcohol content. Czech beers are classified according to the rather complicated Balling scale. A medium-strength Czech beer will be about 4.2 percent alcohol. Never ask for a shandy in Prague – no publican would ever dream of adding lemonade to a beer. If you fancy a change, then try a mixture of a light and dark beer *(řezané pivo)*.

CAFÉS

INSIDER TIP CUKRÁRNA MYŠÁK
(127 F6) *(ɰ G5)*

After the collapse of communism, many traditional cakes and pastries disappeared from the shelves. But now they're back. Once again there is everything a sweet tooth could desire – downstairs ice-cream from a long counter, on the first floor coffee and cakes in an attractive setting. *Mon–Fri 9am–9pm, Sat/Sun 10am–9pm | Vodičkova 31 | metro: Můstek (A, B)*

The café in the Municipal House is a central meeting place

EVROPA ☆ (128 C5) (*G5*)

An enchanting Art Nouveau café in the grand hotel of the same name – with chandeliers and a piano accompaniment. However, you sometimes have to awaken the waiting staff from their slumbers. The guest list ranges from the late Václav Havel to Bulgarian mafia godfathers. Also a nice terrace in the summer. *Daily 7am–midnight | Václavské náměstí 29 | metro: Můstek (A, B)*

INSIDERTIP CAFÉ IMPERIAL (129 D4) (*H3*)

This café and the adjoining hotel have been faithfully restored to their former glory and proudly showcase Prague Art Nouveau architecture. Do stop and admire the high ceilings with their ceramic mosaics. *Daily 7am–11pm | Na poříčí 15 | metro: Náměstí Republiky (B)*

LOUVRE ● (131 E2) (*F5*)

On the first floor and well away from the bustle of the city streets, the Louvre is one of Prague's top coffee houses. In addition to delicious pâtisserie and snacks,

there is also an extensive breakfast menu. INSIDERTIP Billiards is the main activity – usually in the evening – in the stylish side room. *Mon–Fri 8am–11.30pm, Sat/Sun 9am–11.30pm | Národní třída 22 | metro: Národní třída (B)*

INSIDERTIP MONTMARTRE ● (127 E5) (*F4*)

Welcoming cafe with a cosy living-room atmosphere, and despite its proximity to the Royal Way, it is not a tourist trap. Regular guests here have included Franz Kafka, Egon Erwin Kisch and Jaroslav Hašek. Good coffee, draft beer and low prices, but only snacks to eat. *Daily 8am–11pm, Sat/Sun noon–11pm | Řetězová 7 | metro: Staroměstská (A)*

CAFÉ OBECNÍ DŮM ☆ (128 C4) (*G4*)

A magnificent café inside the Municipal House – or outside if the weather's nice. Prague's elite sit alongside short-break tourists, courting couples and pensioners. Highly recommended is the chill counter with its amazing range of cakes.

Daily 7.30am–11pm | Náměstí Republiky 5 | metro: Náměstí Republiky (B)

GRAND CAFÉ ORIENT ● (128 C4) (*🕮 G4*)
The facade of the House of the Black Madonna is not its only Cubist feature. Look inside for proof that an interior in the same style can be both comfortable and relaxing. Coffee and cakes, pancakes and snacks served. *Mon–Fri 9am–10pm, Sat/Sun 10am–10pm | Ovocný trh 19 | metro: Náměstí Republiky (B)*

INSIDER TIP OVOCNÝ SVĚTOZOR (128 C5) (*🕮 G5*)
An ice-cream parlour that is proving very popular with Prague's younger generation. Buy your ice-cream from this ultramodern café, in an arcade off Wenceslas Square, and take it through into the Franciscan Garden. *Mon–Sat 9am–8pm, Sun 11am–8pm | Vodičkova 39 | metro: Můstek (A, B)*

GRAND CAFÉ PRAHA (128 B4) (*🕮 G4*)
A tastefully decorated café and the perfect place to catch up on the day's news. Seats by the window are in demand. You get a close-up view of apostles as they shuffle past the two windows above the Astronomical Clock. *Daily 7am–midnight | Staroměstské náměstí 22 | metro: Můstek (A, B)*

SAVOY (130 C2) (*🕮 E5*)
One of those places where it is important to see and be seen. Top names from Prague's literary circles loved this grand coffee house with its ornate stucco ceiling and large windows; now the well-heeled citizens of Prague drop in to sip their coffee and share the gossip. Great cakes, but its cuisine and wine selection are also highly regarded. *Mon–Fri 8am–10.30pm, Sat/Sun 9am–10.30pm | Vítězná 5 | tram 9, 12, 20, 22: Újezd*

SLAVIA ★ (128 A5) (*🕮 F5*)
Prague's most famous coffeehouse has always been a meeting place for literary types. Despite its popularity with tourists, not much has changed. The biggest plus point in this Art Deco café is its huge window. It offers a spectacular view of the Vltava, the castle and the National Theatre. It's also a good place to eat – with discreet piano accompaniment. Pride of place goes to Viktor Oliva's painting of the 'Absinthe Drinker', in which an intoxicated customer is confronted by a green muse. *Mon–Fri 8am–midnight, Sat/Sun 9am–midnight | Národní třída 1 | tram 9, 18, 22: Národní divadlo*

MARCO POLO HIGHLIGHTS

★ Slavia
Coffeehouse atmosphere with a great view → p. 67

★ Hergetova Cihelna
Tables overlooking the Charles Bridge → p. 68

★ Nebozízek
Treats for the taste buds beneath Prague's Eiffel Tower, accessible by cable car → p. 68

★ Palffy Palác
The perfect place for a romantic meal → p. 68

★ Allegro
There's a fine restaurant in the Four Seasons, plus a delightful terrace → p. 72

★ Aromi
Finest Italian cuisine in Prague's vineyards → p. 72

RESTAURANTS: EXPENSIVE

HANAVSKÝ PAVILON ≤

Pure romance or poor taste? It's a question everyone will have to answer for themselves. Whatever the case, the elaborate, cast-iron pavilion on the Letná hill has a one-off view over the Vltava bridges. Sit and enjoy a coffee on the terrace or choose from a fine menu. *Daily noon–1am | Letenské sady 173 | tel. 2 33 32 36 41 | metro: Hradčanská (A)*

HERGETOVA CIHELNA ★
(127 D4) (*ᗰ E4*)

If you have reserved one of the approx. 150 seats on the ≤ terrace at this converted brickworks, which dates from the 18th century, you will be able to enjoy a stunning view over the Charles Bridge and the Old Town side of the river. Excellent cuisine (Bohemian, Italian and Oriental). *Daily 11.30am–1am | Cihelná 2 b | tel. 2 96 82 61 03 | metro: Malostranská (A)*

NEBOZÍZEK (LITTLE AUGER) ★
(130 B1) (*ᗰ D5*)

This fine restaurant is located right next to the halfway station for the cable-car that goes to the top of Petřín. ≤ Terrace with superb view of the city. Reservation recommended. *Daily 11am–11pm | Petřínské sady 411 | tel. 2 57 31 53 29 | Cable car from Újezd tram stop (nos. 12, 20, 22)*

PALFFY PALÁC ★ (126 C4) (*ᗰ E3*)

Candlelight, piano music and discreet waiters – the place for an intimate dinner for two. Don't forget to book a table! *Daily 11am–11pm | Valdštejnská 14 | tel. 2 57 53 05 22 | metro: Malostranská (A)*

U MODRÉ KACHNÍČKY (THE BLUE DUCKLING) (130 C1) (*ᗰ E4*)

Bohemian cuisine of a high standard at reasonable prices and in a romantic setting. Anything with duck is recommended, but so are all the game dishes. *Daily noon–4pm and 6.30pm–midnight | Nebovidská 6 | tel. 2 57 32 03 08 | tram 12, 20, 22: Hellichova*

WALDŠTEJNSKÁ HOSPODA (WALLEN-STEIN'S) (126 C4) (*ᗰ E3*)

A place where the worlds of politics and business meet. Squeezed between the two chambers of parliament, this luxury restaurant is where all the backroom deals are negotiated. Upmarket Czech cuisine on the menu, game included. *Daily 10am–10pm | Tomášská 20/16 | tel. 2 57 21 29 89 | metro: Malostranská (A)*

LOW BUDGET

▶ You can find the Czech alternative to fast food in the *Zlatý Kříž* delicatessen: *chlebíčky*, thin slices of baguette with various toppings, mayonnaise being an essential ingredient. *Mon–Sat 7am–7pm | Jungmannova 34* **(127 F6)** *(ᗰ G5) | Metro: Můstek (A, B)*

▶ Many pubs and restaurants (even some gourmet restaurants) offer a low-price lunch menu on weekdays from noon to 3pm.

▶ The *Erhartova Cukrárna* pâtisserie sells delicious cakes at low, low prices. *Daily 10am–7pm | Milady Horákové 56* **(128 C1)** *(ᗰ G2) | tram 1, 8, 25, 26: Kamenická*

RESTAURANTS: MODERATE

BREDOVSKÝ DVŮR (132 B1) *(ⓜ H4)*

Tuck into good, solid central European fare, e.g. knuckle of pork or pork ribs with horseradish and sauerkraut. The bar is located in a side street off Wenceslas Square and is very popular with sport fans. A big screen shows all the important football and ice hockey games. In

LVÍ DVŮR (126 B3) *(ⓜ D3)*

Built in 1583, the 'Lion's Court' is situated just before the entrance to the castle. It is said that lions used to be kept in the courtyard, now the speciality is *pražské selátko or* Prague suckling pig. But this elegant spot also serves steaks, vegetarian dishes and fine wines. *Daily 11am–11pm | U Pražného mostu 6/51 | tel. 2 24 37 23 61 | tram 22: Pražský hrad*

Kolkovna – classic Bohemian cuisine washed down with a cool Pilsner Urquell – perfect!

summer you can sit in the inner courtyard. *Mon–Sat 11am–midnight, Sun 11am–11pm | Politických vězňů 13 | tel. 2 24 21 54 28 | metro: Můstek (A, B)*

KOLKOVNA (127 E4) *(ⓜ G3)*

This clean and not too smoky bar near the Old Town Square serves hearty Bohemian specialities, such as špekáčky or bacon sausages, brawn and duck with cabbage. *Daily 11am–midnight | V kolkovně 8 | tel. 2 24 81 97 01 | metro: Staroměstská (A)*

MALOSTRANSKÁ BESEDA (126 C4) *(ⓜ E4)*

Bohemian and international cuisine in a vaulted beer hall setting by the busy *Malostranské náměstí*. Reasonably priced lunch menus also available. *Daily 11am–11pm | Malostranské náměstí 21 | tel. 2 57 40 91 12 | tram 12, 20, 22: Malostranské náměstí*

MOZAIKA (133 E3) *(ⓜ K5)*

Exquisitely presented international cuisine with friendly waiting staff and

LOCAL SPECIALITIES

▶ **Becherovka** – a herbal liqueur from Karlovy Vary, drunk widely in Bohemia and other eastern European countries.

▶ **Pancakes (palačinka)** – a lighter version of the pancake, similar to crêpes, usually served with a filling of marmalade, curd cheese or ice-cream (photo right).

▶ **Pickled Camembert (nakládaný Hermelín)** – a white cheese, which develops a mould on the outside, pickled in oil and garlic. Goes perfectly with beer. One variation is smažený Hermelín, i.e. rolled in breadcrumbs and then deep-fried.

▶ **'Drowned men' (utopenci)** – a classic pub speciality. Sausages are dipped in vinegar, paprika, onions and spices and then served with a slice of bread.

▶ **Potato soup (bramborová polévka)** – not just potatoes, but lots of mushrooms – a heavenly treat when served with fresh bread.

▶ **Dumplings (knedlík)** – usually made from stale bread rolls, plus flour, salt, butter, eggs and milk and then served with meat, game and poultry (photo left).

▶ **Tripe soup (dršťková polévka)** – an authentic Czech Republic speciality, said to be the perfect antidote for a hangover. A thick broth that consists of chitterlings (tripe), usually seasoned with marjoram, pepper and garlic.

▶ **Sirloin of beef (svíčková)** – usually eaten as a festive meal and with a dab of cream added to the lean meat as a final garnish (photo left).

▶ **Moravian meat roll (moravský vrabec)** – comes from Moravia, but is always popular in Bohemia's capital city. The pork shoulder meat is delicious garnished with caraway and garlic. A more correct translation is 'Moravian sparrow'.

▶ **Plum dumplings (švestkovy knedlík)** – at the final stage of preparation they are rolled in breadcrumbs and sprinkled with cinnamon and sugar.

a good selection of wines. Although located in a cellar, it's a stylish restaurant and the ambience is relaxing. Inexpensive lunchtime specials. *Mon–Fri 11.30am–midnight, Sat noon–midnight, Sun noon–11pm | Nitranská 13 | tel. 2 24 25 30 11 | metro: Jiřího Poděbrady (A)*

OLYMPIA (130 C2) (*⊠ E5*)

A modern restaurant serving excellent Bohemian cuisine, with a wide range of beers. If after goulash with dumplings or duck with cabbage you are still hungry, then try a dessert, such as blueberry cake with marzipan. *Daily 11am–midnight | Vítězná 7 | tel. 2 51 51 10 80 | tram 9, 12, 20, 22: Újezd*

POSEZENÍ U ČIRINY (131 F2) (*⊠ G5*)

Small, family-run restaurant with a living-room atmosphere. In charge in the kitchen here is a chef who cooked for ex-president Václav Havel. Menu majors on Czech, Slovak or Hungarian cuisine, including *halušky*, a kind of Slovakian gnocchi with fresh goat cheese. *Mon–Sat 11am–11pm | Navrátilova 6 | tel. 2 22 23 17 09 | metro: Karlovo náměstí (B)*

POTREFENÁ HUSA (THE SHOT GOOSE) (127 E5) (*⊠ F4*)

Stylish bar-restaurant. As long as the high volume and flickering TV screens don't put you off your food, then you will enjoy your meal. On offer are tasty snacks to a more satisfying crispy but succulent goose with cabbage and bacon dumpling. *Sun–Thu 11am–midnight, Fri–Sat 11am–1am | Platnéřská 9 | tel. 2 24 81 38 92 | metro: Staroměstská (A) and also near the Powder Tower (129 D4) (⊠ H4): Sun–Thu 11am–midnight, Fri–Sat 11am–1am | Dlážděná 1003 | tel. 2 24 24 36 31 | metro: Náměstí Republiky (B)*

RETRO (132 C3) (*⊠ J6*)

Generous breakfasts served in this modern restaurant until 11am, good-value menus at lunchtime, in the evening choose between international or Bohemian fare. *Mon–Thu 9am–midnight, Fri 9am–2pm, Sat 1pm–2am, Sun 1pm–10pm | Francouzská 4 | tel. 6 03 17 61 11 | metro: Náměstí Míru (A)*

U SEDMI ŠVÁBŮ (SEVEN SWALLOWS) (126 B4) (*⊠ D4*)

Enter this dimly lit vaulted cellar and sample the best of medieval cooking in the form of hearty, rustic dishes prepared using old Bohemian recipes. Specialities include dripping with greaves, almond vol-au-vent, venison goulash, and, if ordered in advance, suckling pig. Close to the castle quarter. *Daily noon–11pm | Jánský vršek 14 | tel. 2 57 53 14 55 | tram 12, 20, 22: Malostranské náměstí*

RESTAURANTS: BUDGET

BAR BAR (130 C1) (*⊠ E4*)

Stuffed pancakes and a crowded pub – the proprietor calls it the 'ultimate place to eat'. Can a bar that's seemingly always full deceive? Many of his custom-

Bar Bar – always busy

ers come from far and wide just for the pancakes – which are truly the 'ultimate' experience. *Sun–Thu noon–midnight, Fri/Sat noon–2am | Všehrdova 17 | tel. 2 57 31 22 46 | tram 9, 12, 20, 22: Újezd*

BARÁČNICKÁ RYCHTA (126 C4) *(ω D4)*
Is there still a traditional pub in the Lesser Town that is not overrun with tourists? Yes, this is it! In a wood-panelled tavern in the maze of narrow lanes, you can sit alongside the locals and polish off a delicious goulash. *Mon–Sat 11am–11pm, Sun 11–21 | Tržiště 23 | tel. 2 57 53 24 61 | tram 12, 20, 22: Malostranské náměstí*

LEHKÁ HLAVA (LIGHT HEAD) (128 B5) *(ω F4)*
Located in what is said to be Prague's shortest street, this beautifully furnished restaurant serves exclusively vegetarian dishes. No alcohol, just fresh fruit juice. Very tasty! *Mon–Fri 11.30am–11.30pm, Sat/Sun noon–11.30pm | Boršov 2/280 | tel. 2 22 22 06 65 | tram 9, 18, 22: Národní div.*

GOURMET RESTAURANTS

Allegro ★ ≫ (127 D4) *(ω F4)*
When in 2008 the restaurant in the Four Seasons hotel won one Michelin star, it was the first time an eastern European country had received such an award. Unfortunately the Italian chef has since left Prague, but his Czech successor fully intends to maintain the same high standards. A four-course menu will cost about £120/200US$. *Daily 7am–10.30pm | Veleslavínova 2a | tel. 2 21 42 70 00 | metro: Staroměstská (A)*

Aromi ★ (133 D2) *(ω J5)*
News about the quality of this Italian restaurant in the Vinohrady district spread quickly. Haute cuisine, friendly service and a short but constantly changing menu. Recognised for its homemade pasta and excellent fish dishes. Main courses from £15/25US$. Pre-booking essential! *Mon–Sat noon–11pm, Sun noon–10pm | Mánesova 78 | tel. 2 22 71 32 22 | metro: Jiřího Poděbrady (A)*

La Degustation Bohème Bourgeoise (128 C3) *(ω G3)*
Old recipes, modern cooking methods and an abundance of sophistication – two young chefs have arrived here to re-awaken a long-lost tradition – Bohemian cuisine from the Habsburg era. There has long been a gap in the market for this sort of thing. If you would like to sample one of the seven-course menus, you will need plenty of time and about £70/110US$. If you come at lunchtime, it will be whole lot cheaper. *Mon–Sat 6pm–midnight, Tue–Thu also noon–2.30pm | Haštalská 18 | tel. 2 22 31 12 34 | metro: Staroměstská (A)*

Kampa Park (127 D5) *(ω E4)*
The list of celebrities who have eaten here is a long one: Arnold Schwarzenegger, Lou Reed, Václav Havel, Bill Clinton, David Copperfield, to name but a few. The restaurant by the Charles Bridge boasts a stylish ambience and haute cuisine. Main courses from £25/32US$. *Daily 11.30am–1am | Na kampě 8b | tel. 2 96 82 61 12 | metro: Malostranská (A)*

Kampa Park – fine dining with equally fine views of the river

INSIDER TIP LOKÁL (128 C3) (📍 G3)

This is what a typical Czech pub looked like in the 1960s. Austere wooden benches, printed wallpaper, embroidered curtains. The Lokál pays homage to that era, but with two important differences: the waiters are friendly and the food is excellent. Basic Bohemian pub fare made using local ingredients, served with cool, draught Pils lager – what more could you want? *Mon–Fri 11am–1pm, Sat noon–1pm, Sun noon–10pm | Dlouhá 33 | tel. 2 22 31 62 65 | metro: Náměstí Republiky (B) and also in the Lesser Town* (126 C4–5) (📍 E4): *Mon–Fri 11.30am–midnight, Sat noon–midnight, Sun noon–10pm | Míšeňská 12 | tel. 2 57 21 20 14 | tram 12, 20, 22: Malostranské náměstí*

INSIDER TIP U PARLAMENTU ● (128 B4) (📍 F4)

One of the last, down-to-earth Old Town pubs, where Czechs are still in the majority. Simple, very good-value Bohemian cuisine, served with cool Pilsner Urquell. *Mon–Fri 10am–11pm, Sat/Sun 11am–11pm | Valentinská 8 | tel. 7 21 41 57 47 | metro: Staroměstská (A)*

U RUDOLFINA (128 B4) (📍 F4)

The beer keeps flowing here – tasty Pilsner is what draws drinkers to this traditional pub next to the Rudolfinum. But it's good Bohemian cooking that draws guests to the cellar. Don't forget to book a table! *Daily 11am–11pm | Křížovnická 10 | tel. 2 22 31 30 88 | metro: Staroměstská (A)*

ZTRÁTY A NÁLEZY (LOST AND FOUND) (132 C2) (📍 H5)

It may be overflowing with items of lost property, but the young locals who come here are in search of good beer and good food. The cuisine is Bohemian and so is the beer. Reasonably-priced lunch menu. *Daily 11am–11pm | Vinohradská 14 | tel. 2 24 21 63 89 | metro: Muzeum (A, C)*

SHOPPING

CITY **WHERE TO START?**

The city's main shopping artery is **Na příkopě**, which further on becomes **Národní**. If you find there's still not enough choice, then make for **Wenceslas Square**, where there are even more shops, including various clothing chains and the Baťa shoe store. Pařížská or **'Paris Street'** is a miniature version of the Champs-Élysées. It's just a seemingly endless parade of upmarket boutiques selling international fashion brands. Homegrown fashion designers showcase their latest creations a few blocks further on (*Dušní* and *Dlouhá*).

The old favourites are Bohemian crystal, wooden toys and antiquarian books. But things have moved on and shopping in Prague today is all about glitzy malls and exclusive boutiques.

The first stop on your shopping expedition should be *Pařížská,* a tree-lined boulevard noted for its sumptuous Art Nouveau façades. Most of the top fashion brands, such as Hugo Boss, Louis Vuitton and Hermès, have outlets in this elegant street between the Old Town Square and the banks of the Vltava.

Clothes shops for a smaller budget and large book and CD shops are located on Wenceslas Square and along *Národní třída* and *Na příkopě*. Even if you don't want to buy anything, do take a peek

---

Photo: glass and porcelain – traditional souvenirs from the Czech Republic

Books, beer and colourful knick-knacks – you're bound to find something interesting to take home, so do leave some space in your suitcase

inside some of the stores, which occupy grand mansions once owned by Prague's elite (e.g. *Na příkopě no. 4 or no. 8*).

The forerunner of the shopping mall was the arcade and Prague can boast numerous, well-preserved examples from the early 20th century (see Walking Tours, p. 100), but Prague is not stuck in a time warp. For proof of this you need look no further than the Palladium. Clustered together under the roof of an old barracks are some 200 shops and restaurants, linked by spectacular escalators and glass elevators propelling customers up to the retail world's seventh heaven.

If you are looking for traditional Czech souvenirs, then you should stick to the main tourist routes. Puppets, glass, crystal and wooden toys are widely available between the Charles Bridge and the Powder Tower.

You can shop around the clock in Prague, even on Sundays and public holidays.

Bontonland, Prague's largest CD and DVD store, is cloud nine for music fans

BOOKS

ARCO (129 D4) *(∅ H4)*

This short street is home to two antiquarian bookshops (Antikvariát is opposite at no.7), which stock countless rare editions, old photos, film posters and lots more. *Dlážděná 4 | www.antikvariaty.cz | metro: Náměstí Republiky (B)*

INSIDER TIP GLOBE (131 E2) *(∅ F5)*

Is it a bookshop, a café, a cinema or a cabaret? The Globe is pretty well everything – but above all a meeting place for expats, who find the Czech language hard work. *Pštrossova 6 | www.globe-bookstore.cz | metro: Národní třída (B)*

LUXOR (128 C5) *(∅ G5)*

The Palác knih or book palace fully lives up to its name. With around 60,000 titles on shelves spread over four storeys, it is the city's largest bookstore. The foreign language department and the Pragensia section will be of particular interest to tourists. But there is also a good range of art books and children's picture books. *Václavské náměstí 41 | metro: Můstek (A, B)*

VITALIS (126 C4) *(f E3)*

This shop sells books mainly to the German-speaking world, which is entirely appropriate as none other than Franz Kafka, who of course wrote in German, once lived at no. 22 in the Golden Lane. English titles also available. *Zlatá ulička 22 | www.vitalis-verlag.com | Tram 22: Pražský hrad*

CDS & DVDS

BONTONLAND ★ (132 A1) *(∅ G4)*

Prague's largest CD and DVD store. The range is international with sections dedicated to pop, rock, jazz and classical music. Also a special section with recordings by local 'ensembles'. You will also find classic children's films on DVD, e.g.

the 'Mole' series by Zdeněk Miler (1956 onwards). *Václavské náměstí 1 | metro: Můstek (A, B)*

DELICATESSEN

APETIT PRAHA (127 F4) *(ⓜ G3)*
The shop upstairs sells spicy spreads and snacks, downstairs in the clean and welcoming restaurant, they serve tasty fish dishes, including what must be the best fish soup and fish kebabs in town. *Dlouhá 23 | metro: Náměstí Republiky (B)*

AU GOURMAND (127 E4) *(ⓜ G3)*
French cuisine, sweet and savoury, to take away or to eat in, in the tiled bistro café. *Dlouhá 10 | metro: Staroměstská (A)*

INSIDERTIP ▶ JAN PAUKERT
(128 B5) *(ⓜ F5)*
Founded in 1916, this shop's reputation as a purveyor of fine foods is legendary. One counter sells tasty appetisers, the other delicious pâtisserie. There is a wide selection of wines on offer, plus, in the cafeteria at the back, you can get a decent meal at an affordable price. *Národní třída 17 | metro: Národní třída (B)*

PIVNÍ GALERIE (BEER GALLERY)
(0) *(ⓜ K1)*
It may look like a wine merchant's, but it's actually beer bottles on the shelves, in fact some 240 varieties from Czech and European breweries. Not only can you buy the amber liquid, you can also sample it. Opening times can vary! *Tue–Fri noon–1.30pm, 3pm–7pm | U Průhonu 9 | www.pivnigalerie.cz | tram 5, 12: U Průhonu*

ZEMARK (132 A1) *(ⓜ G5)*
The alcoholic drinks on offer tend towards tourists' tastes, but it does also sell a wide range of delicacies. *Václavské náměstí 42 | metro: Muzeum (C)*

GALLERIES

DVORAK SEC CONTEMPORARY
(128 B–C4) *(ⓜ G3)*
This gallery features works by young artists from the USA, Great Britain, Germany and, of course, the Czech Republic. Mainly installations and object art, often comic, sometimes provocative. *Dlouhá 3 | www.dvoraksec.com | metro: Staroměstská (A)*

GALERIE JIŘÍ ŠVESTKA
(129 D3) *(ⓜ H3)*
Not only does this friendly dealer have a weakness for new art from the Old World, he also has an eye for what works. The

---

MARCO POLO HIGHLIGHTS

★ **Bontonland**
Everything from Abba to Zappa on CD → p. 76

★ **Palladium**
Prague's grandest temple of consumption – for everything you could ever want → p. 78

★ **Pohádka**
Toys to make children, and grown-ups, happy → p. 79

★ **Havelský trh**
One of the city's oldest markets → p. 80

★ **Baťa**
Take home a pair of this famous brand's leather shoes from its flagship store → p. 80

★ **Modernista**
'Made in the Czech Republic' but to designs that go back many decades → p. 81

gallery has become an important hub for the art world of eastern, central Europe. *Biskupský dvůr 6 | www.jirisvestka.com | metro: Florenc (B, C)*

GALERIE MIRO (126 A5) (*ΦΦ C4*)
Exhibited in this former chapel are works by such luminaries as Salvador Dalí, and also pictures by amateur artists, notably Karel Gott or Ronnie Wood. Occasionally commercially orientated, but never dull. *Strahovské nádvoří 1 | www.galeriemiro. cz | Tram 22: Pohořelec*

INSIDER TIP ▶ GALERIE ROBERTA GUTTMANNA (127 E4) (*ΦΦ G3*)
This gallery in the Josefov quarter is named after the painter, Robert Guttmann (1880–1942), whose colourful portraits painted a unique chronicle of Jewish life in Prague. Changing exhibitions, often with a Jewish theme. *U Stare školy 3 | www.jewishmuseum.cz/en/agalerie.htm | metro: Staroměstská (A)*

DEPARTMENT STORES

BÍLÁ LABUT' (WHITE SWAN) (129 D3) (*ΦΦ H3*)
Branch of a former Czechoslovakian chain. For a blend of nostalgia and modern times. *Na poříčí 23 | metro: Florenc (B, C)*

KOTVA (ANCHOR) (128 C4) (*ΦΦ G3*)
Freshly renovated and re-stocked, this department store in a 1970s-style steel and concrete construction is successfully defying the stiff competition from the Palladium opposite. 'Made in the Czech Republic' products sold here. *Náměstí Republiky 8 | metro: Náměstí Republiky (B)*

MY NÁRODNÍ (128 B5) (*ΦΦ G5*)
When it opened in 1975 as a Máj store, it won an architectural prize for its striking glass facade and escalators. British visitors may be surprised to see a familiar name above the entrance. Yes, it's a Tesco store and it sells everything you would expect to find in one of its larger UK stores – from clothes to household goods, toys to electrical goods, plus a well-stocked food hall in the basement. *Národní třída 26 | metro: Národní třída (B)*

PALLADIUM ★ ● (128 C4) (*ΦΦ H3*)
During the Habsburg era, it gave shelter to the army, now it markets itself as one of the largest, inner-city shopping centres in Eastern Europe. Within the Palladium you will find some 170 shops and 30 restaurants and bars – including two Starbucks. If you need any convincing that Prague is a thriving, prosperous city, then take a stroll through this temple to consumerism. *Náměstí Republiky 1 | metro: Náměstí Republiky (B)*

SLOVANSKÝ DŮM (SLAVIC HOUSE) (127 F5) (*ΦΦ G4*)
The palace was given its classical look in 1798 and until 1945 it was a 'German casino'. Now this maze is home to shops, restaurants, a cinema and an outdoor bar-restaurant. *Na příkopě 22 | metro: Náměstí Republiky (B)*

ARTS & CRAFTS

ARTĚL (127 F4) (*ΦΦ G4*)
The U.S. designer Karen Feldman established her glass factory in Prague in 1997 and quickly became a trendsetter in the field of Czech crystal glass. Do take a look at her contemporary-style, hand-made glassware. *Rybná 1 | metro: Náměstí Republiky (B)*

DESIGN LOUNGE (128 B4) (*ΦΦ F4*)
Colourful glasses with twisted stems and vases that resemble flowers – Bořek

Šípek's glass art may not be to everyone's taste. But he did have one well-connected patron, namely Václav Havel, who gave him the commission to design part of the castle interior. *Valentinská 11 | www. boreksipek.com | metro: Staroměstská (A)*

MANUFAKTURA ☺ (128 B4) (*Ⓜ F–G4*)
You will find a huge selection of arts and crafts from Bohemia and Moravia here. As you stroll around the city's historic core you will encounter one of its branches at practically every corner.

Mostecká 17 (126 C5) (*Ⓜ E4*) *| tram 12, 20, 22: Malostranské náměstí*

MOSER (128 C5) (*Ⓜ G4*)
Glasses with gold rims, vases with ornate engravings – palaces and mansions belonging to the royal households and the super-rich throughout the world are still adorned with luxury glass vases, bowls and glasses made by this west Bohemian glass and ceramics dynasty. It doesn't cost anything to look! *Na příkopě 12 | metro: Můstek (A, B)*

Puppet on a string – the Good Soldier Švejk is just one of the favourites available from Pohádka

Wide range of goods on offer, from hand-made soap to pottery and paper. It's worth taking a closer look at the traditional wooden toys. Specialities include marble runs, puzzles and characters from 'The Mole' TV series. Tasteful, but affordable. Shops around the Old Town Square include *Melantrichova 17 | Karlova 26 | Železná 3 | metro: Staroměstská (A)*. Shop near the *Malostranské náměstí:*

POHÁDKA (FAIRY TALE) ★ (128 C4) (*Ⓜ G4*)
Literary heroes, such as the Good Soldier Švejk, puppet characters from popular Czech fairy tales, wizards, witches and dragons, but also mechanical toys, dolls' houses, puzzles and jigsaws – it's an Aladdin's cave of gifts for children. *Celetná 32 | metro: Náměstí Republiky (B)*

The Havel market is one of Prague's oldest markets

Pařížská Street near the Čech Bridge ((126 B3) (*ω F3*) | spring until autumn always Sat (until the last Sat in the month) 10am–4pm | metro: Staroměstská (A). To be on the safe side, check dates by consulting www.prazsketrhy.cz.

HAVELSKÝ TRH (HAVEL MARKET) ★ ●
(128 B5) (*ω G4*)
One of the oldest markets of Prague, it is now the place to go for cut-price vegetables, wooden toys of every description and jewellery. If you can't find it here, then you are unlikely to find it anywhere. *Mon–Sat 10am–7pm | Havelská | metro: Můstek (A, B)*

PRAŽSKÁ TRŽNICE (PRAGUE MARKET)
(129 F1) (*ω J2*)
A good place to go for leisurewear, far-eastern electronic gadgetry, toiletries, plus many other odds-and-ends – on the site of an old slaughterhouse. Plenty of fast food stalls. *Mon–Sat 7am–8pm, Bubenské nábřeží 13 | metro: Vltavská (C)*

MARKETS

BLEŠÍ TRH (FLEA MARKETS)
In the northeastern district of Vysočany (0) (*ω 0*) Emil Kolben (1862–1943) ran a company, ČKD (Českomoravská Kolben-Daněk), which built locomotives. Now amid Prague's industrial wasteland you will find Prague's largest flea market, and it is a veritable treasure trove *(Sat/Sun 6am–1pm | Kolbenova | metro: Kolbenova (B)).*
Discarded items from Prague's living rooms can also be found for sale in the small flea market by the river below

FASHION

BAT'A ★ (132 A1) (*ω G4*)
It would be hard to find a town-centre shopping street anywhere in Europe that doesn't have a shoe shop named after the Moravian-born Tomas Bat'a (1876–1932). This vast chain's flagship store can be found on Wenceslas Square – and you are sure to find some great bargains here. *Václavské náměstí 6 | www.bata.com | metro: Můstek (A, B)*

BOUTIQUE TATIANA (129 E4) (*ω G3*)
Tatiana Kovaříková is one of the leading figures in Prague's design circles, with women's fashions in small runs her preference. Simplicity, elegance and femininity are her guiding principles. *Dušní 1 | www.tatiana.cz | metro: Staroměstská (A)*

HANNAH (128 C4) (*∅ G3*)

The Czechs love to get out into the countryside, so there is a strong demand for outdoor clothing. Hannah, a Plzeň-based company, is the largest domestic supplier of jackets, ski suits, hats, gloves, etc. It also sells tents, sleeping bags and rucksacks. *Revoluční 1 | www.hannah.cz | metro: Náměstí Republiky (B)*

HELENA FEJKOVÁ (128 B5) (*∅ G4*)

The boutique run by this fashion designer is not a women-only store. As well as classic-cut outfits and high-class knitwear, there are also collections for men – well-tailored and at affordable prices. *Martinská 4 | metro: Národní třída (B)*

KLÁRA NADEMLÝNSKÁ (127 E4) (*∅ G3*)

After seven years in Paris, in 1997 Klára Nademlýnská began designing luxury garments for women in small runs. Preferring plain colours, her target customers are mainly young people. *Dlouhá 3 | www.klaranademlynska.com | metro: Staroměstská (A)*

BOHEMIAN RETRO (133 E1) (*∅ K4*)

Czechoslovakia lives on here – in the form of clothing, sunglasses, jewellery, porcelain or buttons from the 1930s to 1970s. A retro treasure trove! *Tue–Fri 11am–7pm | Čajkovského 22 | www.bohemianretro.com | metro: Jiřího Poděbrad (A)*

REJOICE (128 C5) (*∅ G–H4*)

Brightly-coloured check cotton fabrics are the trademark of this Czech outdoor fashion house. You will find the message 'made by people in the Czech Republic' on the labels in T-shirts, trousers, caps, shirts and jackets. Colourful, casual gear from this well-stocked store goes down very well with young Czechs. *Jindřišská 17 | www.rejoice.cz | metro: Můstek (A, B)*

JEWELLERY & DESIGN

INSIDER TIP ▶ BELDA (131 E2) (*∅ F5*)

The young team around designer Jiří Belda creates modern jewellery in silver and titanium – some also with colourful appliqué. Clear, geometric shapes are the hallmark of the Belda style. *Mikulandská 10 | www.belda.cz | metro: Národní třída (B)*

MODERNISTA ★ (128 C4) (*∅ G4*)

This is a small shop with a distinctive product range. On sale here are examples of Czech design from the last 100 years, including Cubist porcelain, functional seating and lamps, Art Deco jewellery, modern glassware and designer wooden toys from the 1920s. *Celetná 12 (hidden away in the passage) | www.modernista.cz | metro: Staroměstská (A)*

LOW BUDGET

▶ CDs with Czech labels are still a bargain. Highly recommended souvenirs are classic recordings on the *Supraphon label (www.supraphon.com)*, often with top conductors and performers. If your musical tastes are more contemporary, then take a look at the *Indies* independent label *(www.indies.eu)*, where you will find recordings by avant-garde violinist, singer and composer Iva Bittová or Roma rapper Radoslav Banga, alias Gipsy.cz.

▶ Have a browse around the department stores or craft shops – wooden toys made in the Czech Republic are not only inexpensive, but they are often imaginative and encourage creative play.

ENTERTAINMENT

CITY WHERE TO START?

There are more than enough clubs and bars in every district. If you want to get to know the pub scene away from the tourist trail, you should go to **Žižkov**. Formerly a working-class neighbourhood, it is still a place of smoky dives, where dissidents and non-conformists socialised. Now it's a popular area for young people, creative and alternative types to sit and chat over a beer. Ideally, you should go to a newspaper kiosk and buy a copy of the Czech Republic's English-language newspaper 'Prague Post'. It's got a full 'what's on' listing.

It's hard to imagine that only a few years ago the pavements of Prague would be deserted by 10 o'clock at night. A day in socialist Czechoslovakia began early and ended early. Today you can party around the clock.

In terms of music Prague has something to suit every taste. Classical music lovers should look to see what's on at the Rudolfinum or the Municipal House; if opera is your thing, then there are three different stages to choose from. With jazz too, there is a lot on offer, but the quality is not always great. Prague has a reputation for spawning new and exciting rock bands and there's plenty of variety here too. Good amateur bands often play in smaller venues, such as bars and cellars. And the city by the Vltava is usually on

Top-class entertainment in the form of classical music, clubs, cinema and bars – whatever is your idea of a good night out, you'll find it in Prague

the itinerary of mainstream international bands and singing stars.

The residents of Prague are avid theatre-goers. Admittedly, for tourists, there is a language barrier to overcome, that is, apart from 'black light theatre', where usually no words are spoken. But take care: this art form depends heavily on tourism. If you would like to go to a show, then you should go to the Lanterna Magika, where black light theatre brings film and pantomime together to create an artistic whole. At the cinema, there are fewer language problems, because most international films will be shown in the original, usually with subtitles.

The classic night-out in Prague, however, is a trip to the bar. The words of Bohumil Hrabal (1914–97) are worth bearing in mind on this matter. As a writer of beer-fuelled stories, he was an expert on the theme. For him a bar was a 'small university, where people inspired by beer, recount stories and events, which wound the soul, while above their heads rises the big question mark of absurdity in the shape of cigarette smoke'.

Plenty of room to let yourself go – on the dance floor at the Karlovy Lázně

BARS

BLUELIGHT (126 C4) (*ⓜ E4*)
Countless revellers have scratched messages on the walls of this atmospheric bar. Despite its proximity to the Charles Bridge, the Bluelight has changed little over the years. In fact, for many of Prague's drinkers, it's almost a second home. Sometimes live jazz or funk. *Daily 6pm–3am, Sat/Sun midnight–5am | Josefská 42/1 | tram 12, 20, 22 Malostranské náměstí*

LA BODEGUITA DEL MEDIO (127 E4) (*ⓜ F4*)
This cocktail bar and restaurant in the heart of the Old Town serves a genuine mojito in an authentic Cuban atmosphere. In the lounge guests can become members of Czech Republic's first smokers' club. The 'El Patio' summer garden is also worth a visit. *Tue–Sat 11am–4am, Sun/Mon 11am–2am | Kaprova 5 | metro: Staroměstská (A)*

MONARCH (128 B5) (*ⓜ F4*)
Bohemia is beer country, Moravia is more the land of vineyards and wine drinkers. Czech wine is much improved. Drop in at this pleasant wine bar and check out the local vintages. Plus tasty cheese snacks. Also off-sales of wine. *Mon–Sat 3pm–midnight | Na perštýně 15 | metro: Národní třída (B)*

SOLIDNÍ NEJISTOTA (128 B6) (*ⓜ F5*)
A popular meeting places for the city's VIPs. Distinctive oval bar and crowded dance floor make it the ideal venue for late-night revellers. *Sun–Wed 6pm–4am, Thu–Sat 6pm–6am | Pštrossova 21 | metro: Národní třída (B)*

TRETTER'S BAR (127 E4) (*ⓜ G3*)
A cocktail bar modelled on 1930s New York style; American Michael Tretter has already worked his magic elsewhere in Europe. *Daily 7pm–3am | V kolkovně 3 | metro: Staroměstská (A)*

DISCOS & CLUBS

INSIDER TIP CROSS CLUB
(0) (*0*)

In its early days, it was the haunt only of a few insiders. Now the Cross Club is one of the hottest venues on the 18–25 circuit. From the outside, it's a dilapidated apartment block, on the inside a bold design incorporating industrial scrap metal – with partying on several floors. The programme is a crazy mix of punk concerts, techno DJs, cinema, art and theatre. *Daily 6pm–4am, Fri/Sat until 6am | Plynární 23 | www.duplex. cz | metro: Nadraží Holešovice (C)*

DUPLEX ✸ (127 F6) (*G5*)

It was in this swanky club with restaurant bar and a view over the rooftops of Wenceslas Square that Rolling Stones singer Mick Jagger celebrated his 60th birthday with 200 guests. Where the beautiful people of the night meet up. *Daily 9pm–5am | Václavské náměstí 21 | www.duplex.cz | metro: Můstek (A, B)*

KARLOVY LÁZNĚ (127 D5) (*F4*)

This five-storey dance megalopolis by the Vltava serves up rhythm, red light and rum cocktails. It claims to be the biggest disco in central Europe and has become the first choice for teenagers on school trips. *Daily 9pm–5pm | Novotného lávka | www.karlovylazne.cz | metro: Staroměstská (A)*

INSIDER TIP LUCERNA MUSIC BAR
(132 A2) (*G5*)

The basement of the Lucerna offers everything from techno inferno to tea dance. A classic night-out is the 1980s disco every Saturday evening. *Daily 8pm–3pm | Vodičkova 36 | www.musicbar.cz | metro: Můstek (A, B)*

MECCA (0) (*J1*)

This complex between grey apartment blocks was where Czechoslovakian workers built trams for export. Today the club's dance floors resonate to rock and reggae. Top DJs and one of Prague's coolest spots. *Daily 8pm–5am | U Průhonu 3 | www.mecca.cz | tram 1, 3, 5, 12, 25: Dělnická*

RADOST FX (132 B3) (*H6*)

It describes itself as the 'home of extravagant parties' and some love it, some hate it. When it opened it was the first US-style club in Prague. Noted for its brunch, and there's a gallery in the back-room. Popular among expats, not so much with the locals, but even

---

MARCO POLO HIGHLIGHTS

★ **Lucerna**
A building dating from the days of the silent movie → p. 86

★ **Rudolfinum**
Perfect acoustics mean excellent sound quality → p. 86

★ **U Fleků**
World-renowned watering hole where fraternisation is almost guaranteed → p. 87

★ **U zlatého tygra**
The 'Golden Tiger' is where Bill Clinton went to see a real Czech pub → p. 88

★ **Reduta**
Where jazz caught on in the city by the Vltava → p. 89

★ **Laterna Magika**
Market leader in multi-media matters → p. 91

CINEMAS

so, the music and video shop is almost always packed. *Party Thu–Sat 10pm–3am | Bělehradská 120 | www.radostfx.cz | metro: I. P. Pavlova (C)*

INSIDER**TIP** **RETRO MUSIC HALL**
(132 C3) (*ⓜ J6*)
Reasonable prices, always crowded and popular with the locals – the club has quickly grown into a top venue for Prague partygoers. Innovative programme. *Daily from 7pm, no closing time | Francouzská 4 | www.retropraha.cz | metro: Náměstí Míru (A)*

CINEMAS

AERO (0) (*ⓜ M3*)
Art for art's sake, plus bar. Classic films are shown in their original in the small cinema. Drinks in the bar at very reasonable prices. *Biskupcova 31 | tel. 2 71 77 13 49 | tram 9, 16: Biskupcova*

LETŇÁK (131 D1–2) (*ⓜ E–F5*)
If you are visiting Prague in the summer, then make a point of finding out what's on at the open-air cinema on Marksman's Island (Střelecký ostrov). *July–Aug, films usually start at 10pm | programme: www.letnak.cz | access from the Legií most (bridge) | tram: 9, 12, 20, 22: Újezd*

LUCERNA ⭐ (132 A2) (*ⓜ G5*)
With the eternal appeal of the folding seat – amid such ornate décor in this architectural gem from the 1920s – it's difficult to focus solely on the film. *Vodičkova 36 | tel. 2 24 21 69 72 | metro: Můstek (A, B)*

PALACE CINEMAS (128 C4) (*ⓜ G4*)
There are a total of ten screens with 1,850 seats, so you can watch not just Hollywood blockbusters in Dolby quadraphonic quality, but also the classics from the early years of film history. Proper

popcorn on sale in the foyer. *Na příkopě 22 | tel. 8 40 20 02 40 | metro: Náměstí Republiky (B)*

INSIDER**TIP** **SVĚTOZOR** ●
(131 F2) (*ⓜ G5*)
At the heart of Prague's popcorn-free cinema culture. Programme regularly includes Czech films with English subtitles. There's a small bar in the basement, next to the ticket counter a shop selling movie posters. *Vodičkova 41 | tel. 24 94 2 68 24 | www.kinosvetozor.cz | metro: Můstek (A, B)*

CLASSICAL

CHRÁM SV. MIKULÁŠE
(128 B4) (*ⓜ G4*)
The St Nicholas Church regularly hosts classical music concerts on behalf of the Hussite community. Concerts start either 6pm and 9pm (May–Sept) or 5pm and 8pm (Oct–April) and occasionally at 2pm. *Staroměstské náměstí | tel. 7 74 17 87 74 | metro: Staroměstská (A)*

OBECNÍ DŮM (128 C4) (*ⓜ G4*)
The splendid Smetana Hall in the Municipal House is the home of the Prague Symphony Orchestra. Concerts usually begin at 7.30pm. The auditorium is noted for its superb acoustics. *Náměstí Republiky 5 | tel. 2 22 00 21 01 | metro: Náměstí Republiky (B)*

RUDOLFINUM ⭐ ● (127 E4) (*ⓜ F3*)
The elegant Rudolfinum is the seat of the country's top orchestra, the Czech Philharmonic. Devotees of classical music will want to find time for one of its concerts (usually 7.30pm start), which take place in a superb neo-Renaissance building. *Alšovo nábřeží 12 | tel. 27 05 2 92 27 | www.ceskafilharmonie.cz | metro: Staroměstská (A)*

PUBS

BUKOWSKI'S BAR (129 F5) (*∅ K4*)
A popular pub frequented by expats and Prague's alternative community. *Daily 6pm–3am | Bořivojova 86 | metro: Jiřího z Poděbrad (A)*

LA CASA BLŮ (128 B3) (*∅ G3*)
A little piece of South America in Prague, opened by exiles and students from former fraternal socialist countries. Now a meeting-place that's more living room than bar, but it keeps an impressive collection of rums. *Mon–Fri 11am–midnight, Sat/Sun 2pm–midnight | Kozí 15 | metro: Staroměstská (A)*

U ČERNÉHO VOLA (126 B4) (*∅ C–D4*)
The words of an old folk song say that 'the prettiest girls are to be found in the Black Ox'. That may still be the case, but one thing is certain: the clientele of this old-fashioned bar near the castle are among the thirstiest drinkers in town.

Daily 10am–10pm | Loretánské náměstí 1 | tram 22: Pohořelec

U FLEKŮ ★ (128 B6) (*∅ F5*)
For over 500 years, one of Prague's finest taverns; it can also boast its own dark beer brewery. However, the beer hall and beer garden are nearly always crowded with tourists during the summer. Rather expensive by Prague standards. *Daily 10am–11pm | Křemencova 11 | metro: Národní třída (B)*

INSIDER TIP ▶ FRAKTAL (127 F2) (*∅ G2*)
Cellar bar popular with locals and expats. Always full, always a good atmosphere. Renowned for its succulent burgers. *Daily 11am until at least midnight | Šmeralova 1 | tram 1, 8, 25, 26: Letenské náměstí*

U GLAUBICŮ (126 C4) (*∅ E4*)
Around 1600 Mayor Globic ran a brewery at this spot between the Charles Bridge and the castle; now its Gothic cellar, a smartly-furnished ground floor and

A good head – U Fleků's own brew of dark beer

Live jazz on stage in the legendary Reduta club

an extensive menu continue to draw the crowds. *Daily 10.30am–11pm | Malostranské náměstí 5 | tram 12, 20, 22: Malostranské náměstí*

U VYSTŘELENÝHO OKA (THE SHOT-OUT EYE) (129 F4) (*ⓜ K4*)

Now something of a cult bar in Žižkov, it harks back to the Hussite era – first and foremost to Jan Žižka, the one-eyed warrior of God, who lost his second eye in a battle. It's a smoky dive and nearly always full and you might pass it by if looking for something to eat. In fact you can eat quite well here. One curiosity in the gents' toilet is a headrest above the urinal. *Mon–Sat 4.30pm–1am | U Božích bojovníků 3 | tram 5, 9, 26: Husinecká*

INSIDER TIP U ZAVĚŠENÝHO KAFE (THE HANGING COFFEE) (126 B4) (*ⓜ D4*)

A delightful pub, also with cult status. Tasty, rustic-style food. If a customer's drunk one cup of coffee and he's got some spare cash, he pays for an extra coffee and then hangs an empty cup

above the bar. The next customer who's short of money gets a cup for free. Close to the castle. *Daily 11am–midnight | Úvoz 6 | tram 22: Pohořelec*

U ZLATÉHO TYGRA (THE GOLDEN TIGER) ★ (128 B4) (*ⓜ F4*)

When this traditional-style pub near the Old Town Square opens its doors at 3 o'clock on the dot, there's usually a queue of thirsty customers waiting outside. A loyal band of regulars, one of whom was the great writer and raconteur, Bohumil Hrabal (1914–97). He met former US President Bill Clinton here in 1994. *Daily 3pm until 11pm | Husova 17 | metro: Staroměstská (A)*

LIVE MUSIC

AGHARTA ● (127 E–F5) (*ⓜ G4*)

Intimate club atmosphere à la Manhattan or Chelsea in a cosy cellar near the Old Town Square. Music starts at 9pm. *Daily 7pm–1am | Železná 16 | tel. 2 22 21 12 75 | metro: Můstek (A, B)*

JAZZ DOCK (131 D3) (*∭ E5*)

Modern jazz, experimental and funk. Not in a smoky basement, but in a glass pavilion by the banks of the Vltava – a cool club that attracts local and foreign musicians. *Events usually start at 7pm and/or 10pm | Janáčkovo nábřeží 2 | www.jazzdock.cz | Tram 6, 9, 12, 20: Švandovo divadlo*

KONGRESOVÉ CENTRUM
(132 B6) (*∭ H8*)

The communist government gave little thought to the environment when it built what it called the Palace of Culture, a glass and concrete block popularly known as the White Whale, on a hill overlooking the Vltava. Now used for major events, from classical music to rock. *Ulice 5. května 65 | tel. 2 61 17 11 11 | metro: Vyšehrad (C)*

LIMONÁDOVÝ JOE (127 F4) (*∭ G3*)

This is an unusual alternative club on the top floor of a concrete labyrinth, with retractable roof, cultural programme and snacks. *Daily 10am–3pm | Revoluční 1 |*

Kotva Passage | metro: Náměstí Republiky (B)

INSIDER TIP MALOSTRANSKÁ BESEDA
(126 C4) (*∭ E4*)

Cult house of culture by the Lesser Town Square. Downstairs a pub and café, upstairs a gallery and events hall, with mainly local artists appearing. Many genres, including classical, rock, folk, hip-hop, jazz and experimental, also drama. *Events usually start at 8.30pm | Malostranské náměstí 21 | www.malostranska-beseda. cz | tram 12, 20, 22: Malostranské náměstí*

O2 ARENA (0) (*∭ O1*)

This multi-purpose hall was opened in the spring of 2004. Four floors covering in total 35,000sq m (375,000sq ft) can accommodate up to 18,000 visitors. The Rolling Stones have performed here and it's where Slavia Prague ice hockey team play their home games. *Ocelářská 2 | www. o2arena.cz | metro: Českomoravská (B)*

INSIDER TIP PALÁC AKROPOLIS
(133 E1) (*∭ K5*)

World music, independent, avant-garde – the Akropolis in the trendy Žižkov district is the city's main alternative stage. If there is no band to perform in this former theatre auditorium, then a DJ will fill the void. There is also a bar, a café and almost always an interesting art exhibition. *Daily 7pm–3am, July/Aug 9pm–5am | Kubelíkova 27 | tel. 2 96 33 09 11 | www.palacakropolis.cz | metro: Jiřího z Poděbrad (A)*

REDUTA ★ (128 B5) (*∭ F5*)

The Club Reduta is the acknowledged centre of Prague's jazz scene and is said to be the oldest surviving jazz club in Europe, but experimental jazz is a rare event. If traditional jazz is your thing, then there's something here for you every night. *Daily from 9pm (closes late) | Národní třída 20 | tel. 2 24 93 34 87 | metro: Národní třída (B)*

ROCK CAFÉ (128 B5) *(ψ F5)*

Amateur Czech bands ride the revival wave in this multi-room club. Younger audience. Gigs usually start at 8pm. *Mon–Fri 10am–3am, Sat 5pm–1am, Sun 5pm–1am | Národní třída 20 | tel. 2 24 93 39 47 | metro: Národní třída (B)*

TIPSPORT ARENA (0) *(ψ H1)*

The city's second largest venue for international stars. The grand old hall with seating for 10,000 visitors at the Výstaviště exhibition grounds is also home territory for Sparta Prague ice hockey team. *Za elektrárnou 419 | metro: Nádraží Holešovice (C)*

U MALÉHO GLENNA (126 C5) *(ψ E4)*

Music club downstairs, bar upstairs, catering to a mainly young clientele and casual visitors. Named after the host, the American-born Prague resident by choice, Glenn Spicker. *Daily from 9pm | Karmelitská 23 | tel. 2 57 53 17 17 | tram 12, 20, 22: Malostranské náměstí*

MUSICALS

DIVADLO HYBERNIA (128 C4) *(ψ H4)*

Prague's newest concert hall for musicals. Programme includes a wide range of musicals, usually repeated throughout a season. Prior to its full-scale renovation, this splendid building opposite the Municipal House stood empty for many years. Shows usually start at 7pm, matinées at weekends. *Náměstí Republiky 4 | tel. 2 21 41 94 20 | www.hybernia. eu | metro: Náměstí Republiky (B)*

GOJA MUSIC HALL (0) *(ψ 0)*

Amphitheatre-style layout, so good all-round visibility. This new venue is run by an agency, in which top Czech pop star Karel Gott has a stake. Shows usually start at 7pm, matinées at weekends. *Výstaviště | tel. 2 72 65 83 37 | www.divadlogmh.cz | metro: Nádraži Holešovice (C)*

THEATRE

INSIDER TIP ▶ DIVADLO ARCHA
(129 D4) *(ψ H3)*

Modern stage with refreshing international programme – sometimes well-known, sometimes experimental, but always worth watching. *Na poříčí 26 | tel. 2 21 71 63 33 | www.archatheatre.cz | metro: Florenc (B, C)*

LOW BUDGET

▶ During the summer months the ☆ *beer garden in Letná Park* **(128 C2) *(ψ G2)*** is the place for friends and family to meet up. You collect your ● draft *pivo* from the bar and drink it seated on rather basic wooden benches – but then you do get to enjoy what is probably the finest view over the Old Town and the Vltava. *Letenské sady | tram 1, 8, 25, 26: Sparta*

▶ For many years, clubbers have nominated the former *Roxy* cinema as 'Club of the Year'. This is probably because of the 'free Mondays', when the DJs play for nothing. It's a bit of a maze, but well equipped and there's something for all tastes – from gigs to cult movies. *Daily 7pm–2am | Dlouhá třída 33* **(128 C3) *(ψ G3)*** *| www.roxy.cz | metro: Náměstí Republiky (B)*

DIVADLO NA ZÁBRADLÍ
(128 B5) (*F4*)

The stage where the Czech Republic's former president made his name. Even before 1989, absurd plays by Havel were performed here, and before his death a seat was always kept free for the playwright. Nice theatre bar in the foyer. *Anenské náměstí 5 | tel. 2 22 86 88 68 | metro: Staroměstská (A)*

LATERNA MAGIKA ★ ●
(128 B5) (*F5*)

Although black light theatre now has a number of competitors, this theatre with an unusual facade is still regarded as number one. The magical illusions, which use advanced theatrical skills and video wizardry, are very clever and well worth watching. Incidentally, it was from a back room here that Václav Havel and friends masterminded the Velvet Revolution. *Národní třída 4 | tel. 2 24 93 14 82 | www.laterna.cz | tram 9, 18, 22: Národní div.*

NÁRODNÍ DIVADLO
(NATIONAL THEATRE) (128 B5) (*F5*)

Opera classics, including those by Bedřich Smetana, are performed in this richly-ornamented opera house. An English translation of the lyrics on a display panel accompanies many performances. *Národní třída | tel. 2 24 90 14 48 | www.narodni-divadlo.cz | tram 9, 18, 22: Národní divadlo*

INSIDER TIP SPEJBL & HURVÍNEK
(126 B2) (*D2*)

These father and son dolls have been teasing audiences for over 80 years. A very popular puppet theatre, but it often goes on tour. *Dejvická 38 | tel. 2 24 31 67 84 | www.spejbl-hurvinek.cz | metro: Dejvická (A)*

Mozart's former workplace – the Estates Theatre

STÁTNÍ OPERA (STATE OPERA HOUSE) (132 B2) (*H5*)

Opera usually performed in the language of the original version. *Wilsonova 4 | tel. 2 24 22 72 66 | www.opera.cz | metro: Muzeum (A, C)*

STAVOVSKÉ DIVADLO
(ESTATES THEATRE) (128 C4) (*G4*)

Wolfgang Amadeus Mozart conducted the 1787 première of his 'Don Giovanni' here in this classical theatre. This and other Mozart operas regularly feature on the programme. Orthodox productions faithful to the original. Not a tourist trap. *Ovocný trh 1 | tel. 2 24 90 14 48 | www.narodni-divadlo.cz*

WHERE TO STAY

The red star on the tower is now long gone. But what was once called the Hotel Internacionál still looks as if it has been uprooted from Moscow and moved to Prague. Now it is owned by the luxury hotel chain, Crowne Plaza, and has imposed its high standards on all the rooms – even so, the building's grandiose Soviet style is a stark reminder of Prague's Stalinist era.

But the Crowne Plaza aside, the range of hotels betrays very little of the city's recent past as the capital of a satellite state. There is so much competition. When Prague freed itself from Moscow's control, new hotels opened up in quick succession. Little choice, poor standards and high prices – that's how it used to be. Now there is enough accommodation in

Prague to suit every pocket. Backpacker or luxury traveller – everyone will find something to meet their needs.

Many of the buildings have a tale to tell. There's a former hospital in Baroque style, which has been converted into a hotel. And then there's a medieval and still fully functioning Augustinian monastery, part of which now offers luxury accommodation.

Costs can vary according to seasonal demand. Outside the high season, many hotels offer good value packages, which often beat the budget hostels. At busy periods (April–June, Sept/Oct and New Year), however, don't be surprised to find some rather hefty mark-ups. Prague is a good place to see in the New Year, but if you leave it too late, you may well find that all the city's hotels are full. As a gen-

---

Photo: facade of the Grand Hotel Evropa

A monastery, a former hospital, a tower in Stalinist gingerbread style – accommodation in Prague comes in many forms.

eral rule, book your accommodation over the internet. Not only is it the easiest way to make a reservation, it is also where you will find the best prices.

HOTELS: EXPENSIVE

AMETYST (132 C4) (*ΩΩ H6*)
Austrian-style hotel with pleasant wine bar; quiet location. Restaurants nearby. *87 rooms | Jana Masaryka 11 | tel. 2 22 92 19 21 | www.hotelametyst.cz | metro: Náměstí Míru (A)*

CORINTHIA (132 B6) (*ΩΩ H8*)
A top hotel in every respect – the impressive ☆ glass towers offer excellent views. Bowling and squash. This luxury hotel used to be known as the 'Forum'. *551 rooms | Kongresová 1 | tel. 2 61 19 11 11 | www.corinthia.com | metro: Vyšehrad (C)*

CROWNE PLAZA ★ (0) (*ΩΩ 0*)
Formerly known as the Hotel Internacionál, it is a little bit of Moscow in Prague. In the past, a red star mounted at the top of the tower kept a watchful eye on the

Extravagant – the entrance
to the Hotel Paříž

populace. Built in the 1950s, it has been fully renovated, but many traces of the past remain. *254 rooms | Koulova 15 | tel. 2 96 53 71 11 | www.crowneplaza.cz | tram 8: Podbaba*

DORINT DON GIOVANNI (0) (*N5*)

Futuristic, upmarket hotel by the New Jewish Cemetery. *397 rooms | Vinohradská 157 a | tel. 2 67 03 11 11 | www.dorint. com/prag | metro: Želivského (A)).*

HILTON (129 E3) (*J3*)

A vast, 4-star hotel with a glass lobby. Double rooms from 200 euros. *788 rooms | Pobřežní 1 | tel. 2 24 84 11 11 | www.hilton prague.com | metro: Florenc (B, C)*

HOFFMEISTER ⭐ (127 D3) (*E3*)

An elegantly furnished hotel below the castle, run by descendants of the artist and intellectual Adolf Hoffmeister (1902–73). Numerous caricatures by the master hang in the foyer. A pleasant and friendly atmosphere, plus a new ● spa zone *(daily 9am–10pm, advance booking by phone recommended)*. Guests can now relax in a steam bath in a 15th-century vaulted cavern, which used to be a torture chamber. As well as a Roman-style whirlpool, the spa zone offers a wide range of treatments, even a chocolate massage. *41 rooms | Pod Bruskou 7 | tel. 2 51 01 71 11 | www.hoffmeister.cz | metro: Malostranská (A)*

IMPERIAL (129 D4) (*H3*)

Art Deco tiled walls adorn the fitness suite. The rooms are also decorated in 1920s style and offer every possible comfort. Double rooms from approx. 200 euros. *126 rooms | Na poříčí 15 | tel. 2 46 01 16 00 | www.hotel-imperial.cz | metro: Náměstí Republiky (B)*

INTERCONTINENTAL ⤰ (128 B3) (*F3*)

This luxury hotel by the Vltava, now perhaps showing its age, can boast both an impressive guest list and a fine view over the Old Town. Double rooms from 150 euros. *372 rooms | Náměstí Curieových 43/5 | tel. 2 96 63 11 11 | www.ichotels group.com | metro: Staroměstská (A)*

INSIDER TIP ▶ JOSEF (127 F4) (*G3*)

If you appreciate modern interior design, then you will be perfectly at home in this grand 4-star hotel. Straight lines and bright colours dominate. Only a few yards from the Old Town Square. *109 rooms | Rybná 20 | tel. 2 21 70 01 11 | www.hoteljosef.com | metro: Náměstí Republiky (B)*

INSIDER TIP **KAMPA** ☼ (130 C1) *(Ⓜ E4)*
Idyllic location, welcoming rooms. This quiet, but stylish hotel near the Kampa peninsula and the Charles Bridge is a little gem. *84 rooms | Všehrdova 16 | tel. 2 57 40 44 44 | www.bestwestern-ce.com/kampa | tram 9, 12, 20, 22: Újezd*

MARRIOTT (129 E2) *(Ⓜ H4)*
In a central location with every convenience. Don't be put off by the occasional police presence outside the door – state guests are often accommodated here. *328 rooms | V celnici 8 | tel. 2 22 88 88 88 | www.marriott.com | metro: Náměstí Republiky (B)*

PALACE (128 C5) *(Ⓜ G4)*
Luxury Art Nouveau hotel stylishly furnished; in a side street in the city's historic core. *124 rooms | Panská 12 | tel. 2 24 09 31 11 | www.palacehotel.cz | metro: Můstek (A, B)*

PAŘÍŽ ★ (128 C4) *(Ⓜ G4)*
A 5-star hotel in the Old Town, dating from 1904. Guests always appreciate the spacious rooms; an impressive Art Nouveau exterior. *102 rooms | U Obecního domu 1 | tel. 2 22 19 51 95 | www.hotel-paris.cz | metro: Náměstí Republiky (B)*

SAX ★ (126 B4) *(Ⓜ D4)*
Retro interior in 1960s style, within a classical-style exterior; in the Lesser Town's embassy quarter. *22 rooms | Jánský vršek 328 | tel. 2 57 53 12 68 | www.sax.cz | metro: Malostranská (A)*

THE 987 PRAGUE HOTEL
(129 D4) *(Ⓜ H4)*
Design hotel with high-quality service in a central location. *80 rooms | Senovážné náměstí 15 | tel. 2 55 73 72 00 | www.987-praguehotel.com | metro: Náměstí Republiky (B)*

HOTELS: MODERATE

AMEDIA TEATRINO
(133 E1) *(Ⓜ K4)*
Formerly a theatre in the Žižkov bar quarter, it is now a lovely 4-star hotel, where the interior designers paid loving attention to detail. *73 rooms | Bořivojova 53 | tel. 2 21 42 21 11 | www.amediahotels.com | tram 5, 9, 26: Lipanská*

ANNA (133 D3) *(Ⓜ J6)*
Small, clean hotel in the Vinohrady district. Lots of restaurants and small, 'open-all-hours' shops nearby. *24 rooms | Budečská 17 | tel. 2 22 51 31 11 | www.hotelanna.cz | metro: Náměstí Míru (A)*

AXA (129 D3–4) *(Ⓜ H3)*
Functional hotel with a spa zone, in the town centre. *138 rooms | Na poříčí 40 | tel. 2 27 08 51 11 | www.hotelaxa.cz | tram 3, 8, 24: Bílá Labuť*

★ **Crowne Plaza**
Luxury hotel in Stalinist gingerbread style → p. 93

★ **Hoffmeister**
Art and design together under one roof → p. 94

★ **Paříž**
Art Deco flagship in the Old Town → p. 95

★ **Sax**
Design hotel with a light and airy atrium → p. 95

★ **The Augustine**
Stay the night in a monastery, but enjoy all the comforts of a luxury hotel → p. 96

MARCO POLO HIGHLIGHTS

DAVID (131 E3) (*Ⓜ F5*)
Ultra-modern and tastefully-furnished 4-star hotel not far from the Charles Square (Karlovo *náměstí*). Stylish, but still affordable. *76 rooms | Náplavní 6 | tel. 222 516 150 | www.eurostarsdavid. com | metro: Karlovo náměstí (B)*

INSIDERTIP▸ DŮM U VELKÉ BOTY
(126 B5) (*Ⓜ D4*)
A well-run family guesthouse, the 'House of the Large Shoe' does not have a hotel sign, just 'Rippl', the name of the proprietor by the doorbell. All the rooms in this tastefully-renovated hotel are individually furnished and very cosy. In a quiet spot opposite the German embassy. *8 rooms | Vlašská 30 | tel. 257 53 20 88 | www.du muvelkeboty.cz | metro: Malostranská (A)*

EVROPA (128 C5) (*Ⓜ G6*)
The fine Art Nouveau interior of this 2-star hotel has been enchanting guests since 1905. Adjoining café in Viennese style. However, some rooms in urgent need of renovation. *92 rooms | Václavské náměstí 25 | tel. 224 215 387 | www. evropahotel.cz | metro: Můstek (A, B)*

INSIDERTIP▸ HOTEL 16 (131 F3) (*Ⓜ G6*)
This is one of Prague's best-kept secrets, a plush hotel near the city centre; small

LUXURY HOTELS

The Augustine ★ (126 C4) (*Ⓜ E3*)
A luxury hotel chain and an Augustinian monastery have signed up to a joint venture. Monks live in one part of the complex, while well-heeled guests from all over the world are lavishly indulged in the other part. An elegant hotel with furnishings in Czech Cubist style. The former dining room in the monastery is now a bar, likewise the former brewery. If you would like to see inside the historic monastery library, you should ask one of the friars for a viewing. Double rooms from approx. 10,000 Kč. *117 rooms | Letenská 12/33 | tel. 2 66 11 22 33 | www.theaugustine. com | metro: Malostranská (A)*

Carlo IV. (129 D4) (*Ⓜ H4*)
Lavishly renovated neoclassical palace in a central location not far from Wenceslas Square. Double rooms from approx. 5,000 Kč. *152 rooms | Senovážné náměstí 13 | tel. 2 24 59 31 11 | www.* *prague.boscolohotels.com | metro: Hlavní nádraží (C)*

Four Seasons (127 D5) (*Ⓜ F4*)
This hotel complex by the Vltava consists of three historic buildings and one new one, which caused quite a stir, when it was built. Now most people find the styles blend together well. Double rooms from approx. 9,500 Kč. *161 rooms | Veleslavínova 2 a | tel. 2 21 42 70 00 | www.fourseasons.com | metro: Staroměstská (A)*

Mandarin Oriental (126 C5) (*Ⓜ E4*)
A 14th-century monastery that has been transformed with great care into a first-class hotel. Idyllic location in the Lesser Town. Double rooms from approx. 9,000 Kč. *99 rooms | Nebovidská 459/1 | tel. 2 33 08 88 88 | www.mandarin oriental.com/prague | tram 12, 20, 22: Hellichova*

rooms, great service. You can eat well in the JB Club restaurant nearby. *14 rooms | Kateřinská 16 | tel. 2 24 92 06 36 | www. hotel16.cz | metro: Karlovo náměstí (B)*

JELENÍ DVŮR (126 A2) (*ⓓ C3*)
Only a few minutes' walk from the castle; small hotel with a friendly atmosphere. Pets welcome. *30 rooms | Jelení 197 | tel. 2 33 02 83 33 | www.hotel-jeleni-dvur. info | tram 22: Brusnice*

MAMAISON RESIDENCE BELGICKÁ (132 C4) (*ⓓ H6*)
Smart aparthotel in a quiet side street in the gentrified Vinohrady district. Lots of restaurants in the vicinity, plus metro and tram stops within a stone's throw. 30 apartments all with modern kitchenettes. *Belgická 12 | tel. 2 21 40 18 00 | www.mamaison.com | metro: Náměstí Míru (A)*

OPERA (129 D3) (*ⓓ H3*)
Said to be the oldest hotel in Prague (established 1891), but it is ageing well. Friendly atmosphere. Pets welcome. *67 rooms | Těšnov 13 | tel. 2 22 31 56 09 | www.hotel-opera.cz | metro: Florenc (B, C)*

PYRAMIDA ☆ (0) (*ⓓ B4*)
A modern, but perhaps rather faceless hotel complex behind the castle. *354 rooms | Bělohorská 24 | tel. 2 33 10 22 71 | www.hotelpyramida.cz | tram 15, 22, 25: Malovanka*

QUESTENBERK (126 A4) (*ⓓ C4*)
The entrance looks like a Baroque church, but during the 17th century this hotel close to the castle was a hospital. Plain but elegant furnishings. Fine location on Petřín Hill overlooking the city. *33 rooms | Úvoz 15 | tel. 2 20 40 76 00 | www.hotelq.cz | tram 22: Pohořelec*

Grand Hotel Evropa – a light and elegant atrium

HOTELS: BUDGET

A&O HOSTEL (0) (*ⓓ H1*)
This no-frills chain now has a place in Prague. Basic single, double and multi-bed rooms, handy location for public transport near Holešovice station. Opposite the exhibition grounds and the extensive Stromovka Park. No breakfast. *31 rooms | U Výstaviště 1/262 | tel. 2 20 87 02 52 | www.aohostels.com/de | metro: Nádraží Holešovice (C)*

Smart but affordable – the Czech Inn won a design award

ADALBERT ☺ (0) (*⊞ 0*)

Waste separation, locally-sourced food and no unnecessary towel replacement. Environmental issues respected in this hotel on the site of the 1,000-year-old Břevnov Monastery. Simple rooms, generous buffet breakfast. *25 rooms | Markétská 1 | tel. 2 20 40 61 70 | www.hoteladalbert.cz | tram 15, 22, 25: Břevnovský klášter*

ANDANTE (128 C6) (*⊞ G5*)

As well as a restaurant, this hotel can also supply tourist guides and a shuttle service to and from the airport. Central, clean and friendly. Book online. *32 rooms | Ve Smečkách 4 | tel. 2 22 21 00 21 | www.andante.cz | metro: Muzeum (A, C)*

BALKÁN (131 D4) (*⊞ E6*)

Affordable hotel near the river. By a busy road, so when booking ask for a room overlooking the courtyard. *31 rooms | Svornosti 28 | tel. 2 57 32 71 80 | www.hotelbalkan.cz | metro: Anděl (B)).*

INSIDER TIP ▶ CZECH INN
(133 D4) (*⊞ K6*)

This hostel was awarded a design prize and was also included in the Washington Post's list of the 12 best big city hotels. *130 beds (single and double rooms) | Francouzská 76 | tel. 2 67 26 76 00 | www.czech-inn.com | tram 4, 22: Krymská*

MISS SOPHIE'S HOSTEL
(132 A–B3) (*⊞ G6*)

Very clean hotel with modern furnishings. Basic but adequate facilities, nice atmosphere and central location. *30 beds (single and double rooms) | Melounova 3 | tel. 2 96 30 35 30 | www.miss-sophies.com | metro: I.P. Pavlova (C)*

RESIDENCE 4
(128 C1) (*ΩΩ G1*)

Inexpensive apartments for two to six people, in a good location. Not a design masterpiece, but neat, tidy and practical. *22 rooms | Umělecká 4 | tel. 2 33 35 94 88 | www.residence4bandb. com | tram 1, 8, 25, 26: Kamenická*

SIR TOBY'S HOSTEL
(129 F1) (*ΩΩ K1*)

Perfectly acceptable guesthouse for the not too discerning guest, near Holešovice main-line station. *12 rooms | Dělnická 24 | tel. 2 46 03 26 10 | www.sir tobys.com | tram 1, 3, 5, 12, 25: Dělnická*

STANDARD (131 E4) (*ΩΩ F7*)

Art Nouveau hotel by the Vltava south of Palackého náměstí; ☼ most rooms have a castle view. *11 rooms | Rašínovo nábřeží 38 | tel. 2 24 91 60 60 | www. standard.cz | tram 3, 16, 17, 21: Výtoň*

TREVI (132 C3) (*ΩΩ J6*)

Small and basic hotel in the 19th-century Vinohrady quarter; lots of restaurants and bars nearby. *18 rooms | Uruguayská 20 | tel. 7 22 81 10 97 | www.praguehotel trevi.com | metro: Náměstí Míru (A)*

UNION (132 A5) (*ΩΩ G7*)

Inconspicuous building, hidden away under the Nusle Bridge. Small rooms with well-stocked minibars. Private parking on site, many eateries nearby. *57 rooms | Ostrčilovo náměstí 4 | tel. 2 61 21 48 12 | www.hotelunion.cz | tram 7, 18, 24: Ostrčilovo náměstí*

OTHER ACCOMMODATION

CAMPING (0)

Most of the campsites on the outskirts of the city are clean and well-equipped. Before booking a pitch, enquire about the electrical voltage offered. *Oase Praha | Zlatníky 47 | www.campoase.cz; Sokol Trója | Trojská 171a (ΩΩ F8) | www.camp-sokol-troja.cz; Císařská Louka | Císařská louka 162 | www.caravancamping.cz*

EASY TRAVEL
(129 D5) (*ΩΩ H4*)

First point of contact if you are looking for a hotel or privately-run accommodation. *Daily 6am–11pm | in the main station | Wilsonova 8 | tel. 7 73 55 00 08 | www.prague agency.com | metro: Hlavní nádraží (C)*

LOW BUDGET

▶ Admittedly, the Lesser Town Square is not exactly a tranquil spot, but it's in the heart of the historic core and where most of the action is. At only 450 Kč per person, the Little Town Budget Hotel is a clean place to rest your head. *Malostranské náměstí 11* **(126 C4)** *(ΩΩ E4) | tel. 2 42 40 69 64 | www.littletownhotel.cz*

▶ Basic, but very popular with young people is the Traveller's Hostel. Central, but not particularly quiet. Double room including breakfast costs 750 Kč. Breakfast, multi-bed rooms from 350 Kč per person. *164 beds | Dlouhá 33* **(128 C3)** *(ΩΩ G3) | tel. 2 24 82 66 62 | www.travellers.cz | metro: Náměstí Republiky (B)*

▶ As a general rule, book early and online and you will get the best prices. The internet portal *www.prague. st* offers good value special deals in hotels of all categories, e.g. double rooms in central, but clean and tidy hotels from 1,000 Kč.

WALKING TOURS

The tours are marked in green in the street atlas,
the pull-out map and on the back cover

1 TAKE A STROLL THROUGH THE SHOPPING MALLS OF YESTERYEAR

You should allow two hours for this tour of Prague's indoor arcades
'A stranger walks the streets, a local will use an arcade, if it shortens his route or if he wants to impress a lady from the countryside with his knowledge of the big city,' wrote the Czech writer and journalist Egon Erwin Kisch in 1920. Prague is not exactly renowned for its arcades, in fact not many people know of their existence. But these often ornate shortcuts in the city by the Vltava are just a little bit special. They are delightfully antiquated; there's a whiff of nostalgia, of a bygone age.

The starting point for a tour of Prague's pasáže is on **Wenceslas Square** → p. 59 at the entrance to the INSIDER TIP *Lucerna Arcade (Štěpánská 61)*. This edifice, Prague's the first reinforced concrete structure, was built in Prague between 1907 and 1921 by Václav Havel, the grandfather of the Czech Republic's long-serving president. Beneath the palace is an intricate maze of passageways with cinemas, shops and restaurants; in the basement there's even a ballroom, where Karel Gott performs his Christmas concerts. If you'd just like to watch the world go by, order a coffee in the Lucerna Café (in the cinema foyer on the first floor) and find a table beside one of the large windows. From here you can also get a close-up of one of a number

Photo: arcade in the Koruna Palace on Wenceslas Square

Amble through nostalgic shopping arcades or climb wooded slopes – how to explore one of Europe's finest capital cities on foot

of wry observations on national pride by the Prague artist David Černý. St Wenceslas sits astride the chest of an inverted horse – a post-modern counterpart to the equestrian statue of the country's patron saint on Wenceslas Square.

The rear of the Lucerna opens on to Vodičková and immediately opposite is the entrance to the Světozor Arcade (Vodičková 39). This constructivist building dates from 1928. One major attraction inside is the Světozor → p. 67 ice-cream parlour. There's also a shop

for stamp collectors here. Hidden away around the corner is a green and pleasant retreat, the Franciscan Garden → p. 54. Laid out in 1950 and with a statue-studded fountain, it's where groups of Prague office workers gather for a chat during the lunch break.

A gravel path leads past the Gothic Church of our Lady of the Snows > p. 54 to Jungmannovo náměstí. Work on the church started in 1379 and it was intended to have three naves and be more than 100m in length. It didn't happen. Had it done so, it would have taken over what is now the Jungmannovo náměstí. From the statue of the Slavic philologist, Josef Jungmann (1773–1847), which gave the square its name, you now cross into the **Adria Arcade** *(Jungmannova 35)*. This late Cubist building in the style of a Venetian Renaissance palace was built in 1924 as the head office for an insurance company. As well as some nice shops, it is also home to a good restaurant and a theatre. At one time the famous black light theatre, **Laterna Magika** → p. 55 was based here. The facade is adorned with sculptures and a sundial by the respected sculptors, Otto Gutfreund and Bohumil Kafka. Also rather striking is the **maritime statue** by Jan Štursa (1924). An architects' guide to Prague once wrote that the Adria Palace is reminiscent of 'an extravagant wedding cake' and it does indeed contrast starkly with the functional ARA building opposite. You then emerge on **Národní třída** (National Avenue) and are back in the bustling city centre. However, only 100m down the road, on the other side, beyond no. 37, a narrow alley crosses via the **Platýz courtyard** to **Uhelný trh** (Coal Market). The Platýz was built in the middle of the 13th century on the site of the city wall (remains of which can still be seen in the cellar). After alterations in the mid-19th century, it became one of Prague's first apartment blocks. In fact Franz Liszt stayed here in 1846 (see the memorial plaque at the entrance to Uhelný trh). In 1419 in the neighbouring church of **St Martin in the Wall**, Hussites first offered goblets with communion wine to the faithful, thereby proclaiming their opposition to the Catholic Church. After restoration work on a grand scale, Uhelný trh was re-opened in its present form in the winter of 1998/99. It was at no. 420 that Wolfgang Amadeus Mozart lived in 1787 and a plaque recalls his time in the city. It would not a have been a pretty view from his window, because below in the middle of the square was

The Franciscan Garden – in the background the nave of the Church of Our Lady of the Snows

the market where until 1807 coal and charcoal were traded. Today the **Wimmerova fountain** dominates the square. This classical piece, the work of sculptor Frantisek Xaver Lederer, bears allegorical references to viticulture. It was made for the patron of the arts, Jakob Wimmer, who donated it to the city. In 1951 when Národní třída was redesigned, the fountain was moved here.

This walk ends at Uhelný trh. If you are need of a rest and some liquid refreshment, then you could call in for a beer at **U dvou koček** (Two Kittens) in the arcade. If you would like to explore even more of Prague's hidden arcades, then seek out the **Jalta Arcade** and the **Koruna Palace,** at the top end and bottom end of Wenceslas Square respectively.

2 THROUGH THE NEW TOWN IN HONOUR OF DVOŘÁK AND ŠVEJK

A lot has changed since Charles IV laid out this part of the city in 1348. What has survived is a mix of townhouses and grand dwellings built for status-conscious merchants – allow a good three hours for the walk. The journey back in time begins at the **museum** → **p. 53** dedicated to the Czech's national composer, **Antonín Dvořák** (1841–1904). It is actually a Baroque summer palace *(Ke Karlovu 20)* designed in 1712 by Kilian Ignaz Dientzenhofer and bears the name 'Amerika' in memory of the time Dvořák spent at the Conservatory in New York (1892–95). On display in the museum, in what was the study, are numerous papers documenting his life and work.

Just around the corner *(Na bojišti)* is a museum dedicated to another great Praguer, the Good Soldier Švejk. Soldier Švejk regularly drank with his comrades in the **U kalicha** (The Goblet). Or at least

The Good Soldier Švejk

that is how it is recounted by Jaroslav Hašek, the author of the celebrated, comic novel set during World War I. Hašek was himself one of the regulars in the 'Goblet', whose walls are decorated with the famous Švejk illustrations by Josef Lada.

If you follow Kateřinská in the direction of the Vltava, you will cross hospital grounds, which resemble a park. The Late Empire building in the centre was constructed in 1787, and then in subsequent years the site was extended to include gardens and outbuildings. The whole area is now something of a 'town within a town'.

Pass the Science Faculty buildings of the Charles University *(Viničná)* and the Church of St Apollinarius, a church commissioned by Charles IV, and continue down *Apolinářská*. On *Na slupi* at the end is the much-visited INSIDER TIP *Botanical Garden (entrance on the corner of Benát-ská)*. It depends on the time of year, but among its highlights are a fine display of flowering cacti and a collection of exotic birds. This spacious outdoor area with numerous greenhouses was established in 1845. It replaces the garden, which a botanist from Florence laid out at the behest of Charles IV.

Continue towards the river *(Trojická, Pod Slovany)* and rising up on the right-hand side, you will see the ● **Emmaus Monastery** with the adjoining Church of Our Lady, yet another church that Charles IV had built. The monastery was founded in 1347 for Slavic Benedictine monks. Its architectural style reflects the history of the New Town: the monastery was 'baroquised' between 1636 and 1880 and then restored to its original Gothic style; during the 20th century, the roof was rebuilt with a reinforced concrete structure of twin spires in a daring 'crossover' design. Look out for the Gothic frescoes in INSIDER TIP **the cloister**.

If you now follow *Na moráni*, you will eventually arrive at the showpiece of Charles IV's far-sighted town plan, **Charles Square**. For many years the city's cattle market, it is now Prague's largest square (350m by 150m), in fact it's now more a park than a square. On the south side at no. 40 stands the **Faust House**, where the English alchemist Edward Kelley lived in the late 16th century.

③ PETŘÍN – A GREEN REFUGE OPPOSITE THE OLD TOWN

The people of Prague used to cultivate the vineyards and work the quarries on ★ Petřín Hill. Today it is a popu-

lar destination for a Sunday outing – and if you follow this route it will take around two hours.

The walk begins at **Náměstí Kinských**. Stands of hundred-year-old trees lead up to a spacious grassy area that was created in 1825.

At the upper end is the **Kinský Summer Palace**. Behind this impressive Empire building, a wooden bell tower from Wallachia and then, a little further on in the park, a wooden church, exemplify Moravian folk art. What is known as the **Hunger Wall** (1360) lines the route to the top of the hill. According to legend, Charles IV ordered its construction as part of the city's fortifications after a poor harvest. Thousands of starving people worked on it, in return they received food from the royal stores.

A 63-m (200-ft) high ☼ **mini-Eiffel Tower** affords a fantastic view over the city. Built in 1891, this iron structure with 299 steps is indeed a replica of the Paris original *(April–Sept daily 10am–10pm,*

Oct/March daily 10am–8pm, Nov–Feb daily 10am–6pm | admission 100Kč). Dating from the same year is the nearby **INSIDER TIP** **Mirror Maze** → p. 106. The building also houses a 90sq m (950sq ft) diorama, illustrating the brave fight that Prague students put up on the **Charles Bridge** → p. 47 defending the city from Swedish troops in 1648.

There are several ways down from the top of the 327-m (1,075-ft) high Petřín Hill. Either head down through the woods towards Vlašská or follow a footpath through the Hunger Wall to the **Růžový sad** (Rose Garden). However, many prefer the nearby **INSIDER TIP** **funicular railway**, which drops 511m (1,675ft) down to Újezd metro station. A ride down the gentle slope is fun and the view from the cabin over the historic Old Town is stunning. If you do decide to head down to Vlašská, then you can see a building that helped to change the course of European history. At the foot of Petřín is **Lobkowicz Palace**, since 1975

the home of the then West German embassy. In the autumn of 1989, thousands of East Germans managed to reach the grounds of the embassy and demanded exit visas to West Germany. The most memorable event, however, was the appearance there on 30 September 1989 of Hans-Dietrich Genscher, the West German Foreign Minister. In a moving address, he announced from the balcony to the refugees living in the tent city that they would be granted exit permits. No one ever heard the entire sentence. He started it with the words 'We have come to you to tell you that today your departure …' but the last part was drowned out by cheers. A quirky piece by David Černý in the embassy garden recalls these historic moments. The Prague artist created a Trabant car on legs. Popularly known as 'Trabbis', these cheap and cheerful cars with a resin body were made in East Germany and exported widely throughout the eastern bloc during the communist era.

The Charles Bridge links the Old Town with the Lesser Town below Hradčany

TRAVEL WITH KIDS

They say Prague is not a city of museums, but a museum in itself. But don't be misled. Children will also find lots of interesting things to do here. They love the 19th-century cable-car up Petřín Hill, for example. And once they get there, it's not far to the historic **INSIDERTIP** *Mirror Maze (Bludiště)*, which is always a winner with youngsters. *(April–Sept daily 10am–10pm, Oct/March daily 10am–8pm, Nov–Feb daily 10am–6pm | admission 70Kč)*.

CHILDREN'S ISLAND
(DĚTSKÝ OSTROV) (131 D2–3) (*ᗰ E5*)
There's an island in the Vltava dedicated to children. Playgrounds and climbing frames for the little ones, skateboard ramps and a mini-football pitch for the older ones. *April/Oct 9am–8pm, Nov–March 10am–5pm | entrance from Janáčkovo nábřeží on the left bank | tram 6, 9, 12, 20: Arbesovo náměstí*

PLANETÁRIUM (0) (*ᗰ G1*)
Children love Stromovka Park and not just for the inline skating, cycling and games, but also for the Planetárium. The slide and video shows bring the heavens just that little bit nearer, even if most of the presentations are in Czech. But there are regular guided tours in English. More than 200 people can be accommodated in the main hall beneath a simulation of the galaxies. A real star trek! *Mon 8.30am–noon and 1pm–6pm, Tue–Thu 8.30am–noon and 1pm–8pm, Sat 9.30am–noon and 1pm–8pm, Sun 9.30am–noon and 1pm–6pm | admission 60–160Kč | Královská obora 233 | www.planetarium.cz | tram 5, 12, 14, 17: Výstaviště*

TOY MUSEUM (MUZEUM HRAČEK)
(126 C4) (*ᗰ E3*)
The exhibition rooms on the castle site are packed full of tin cars and trains, furry animals and dolls, even Barbies. An array of glass cabinets contains a huge collection of toys, a few dating from ancient Greece, most from modern times. *Daily 9.30am–5.30pm | admission 60Kč, family ticket 120Kč | Jiřská 6 | Metro: Malostranská (A)*

NATIONAL TECHNOLOGY MUSEUM
(NÁRODNÍ TECHNICKÉ MUZEUM)
(128 C2) (*ᗰ G2*)
This museum is anything but dusty. Before you're past the entrance hall, you'll be overwhelmed by cars, planes and locomotives and you won't see lots of 'Please do not touch' signs. Visitors can

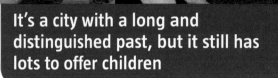

It's a city with a long and distinguished past, but it still has lots to offer children

climb into the cab of a steam engine or type on a manual typewriter. *Tue–Sun 10am–6pm | admission 170Kč, family ticket 370Kč | Kostelní 42 | tram 1, 8, 25, 26: Letenské náměstí*

TRANSPORT MUSEUM (MUZEUM MĚSTSKÉ HROMADNÉ DOPRAVY)
(126 A3) (*ĐĐ C3*)

Punctual and reliable – you really can't complain about Prague's trams, unless perhaps you are travelling with a pushchair and are having to cope with stairs and inconvenient doorways. Most children enjoy riding on the trams, which rattle through the city centre. If they would like to see more *tramvaj* models, underground carriages and trolley buses, then the Museum of Transport always gets a good reception. Over 40 vehicles are exhibited in the historic depot – and that includes a horse drawn tram from 1886. You don't have to visit the Transport Museum to use the 'Nostalgia Tram' *(35Kč)*, which starts from the museum

and does a circular tour via Wenceslas Square, the Lesser Town and the castle. You can get on and off at any stop. *April–Nov Sat/Sun 9am–5pm | admission 35Kč | Patočkova 4 | tram 1, 18, 25: Vozovna Střešovice*

ZOO (ZOOLOGICKÁ ZAHRADA)
(0) (*ĐĐ 0*)

More than 650 animal species, including gorillas, warthogs, giraffes and penguins, can be seen on a sprawling site, crisscrossed by natural streams and dotted with rocks. If you're feeling lazy, you can take a chair lift up to the higher level. Here's a useful tip: rather than take the bus from the city centre, take a river cruise to the zoo *(Rašínovo nábřeží | 150Kč | departures May –Sept 9am and noon)*. June–Aug daily 9am–7pm, April/ May/Sept/Oct 9am–6pm, Nov– March 9am–4pm | admission 150Kč, family ticket 450Kč | U Trojského zámku 3/120 | bus no. 112 from Nádraží Holesovice metro station (C) | www.zoopraha.cz*

FESTIVALS & EVENTS

PUBLIC HOLIDAYS

1 Jan: *New Year;* **Easter Monday; 1 May:** *May Day;* **8 May:** *End of World War II;* **5 July:** *St Cyril and St Methodius Day;* **6 July:** *Death of Jan Hus in Constance 1415;* **28 Sept:** *St Wenceslas Day;* **28 Oct:** *Republic Day;* **17 Nov:** *Struggle for Freedom and Democracy Day;* **24–26 Dec:** *Christmas*

EVENTS

JANUARY

▶ *New Year Concert:* Top-class performances at various venues at various times throughout New Year's Day. People in the know say that the Prague Symphony Orchestra's concert in the *Municipal House (Obecní dům) is the best. Metro: Náměstí Republiky (B)*

▶ INSIDER TIP *New Year fireworks displays:* Hotels and families celebrate on New Year's Eve, the city celebrates on New Year's Day. It usually starts at 6pm.

FEBRUARY

▶ *Holiday World:* Grand holiday and leisure trade fair at *Výstaviště exhibition grounds. Metro: Nádraží Holešovice (C)*

MARCH

▶ *St Matthew's Fair:* Prague's oldest funfair at the *Výstaviště fairground site. Metro: Nádraží Holešovice (C)*

▶ *Febiofest:* International film festival at the end of March with famous actors and producers in attendance. *www.febiofest.cz*

MAY/JUNE

▶ ★ *Prague Spring Festival:* An important event in the classical music calendar. Between mid-May and mid-June top international musicians perform in Prague. Get your tickets in good time! *Obecní dům | metro: Náměstí Republiky (B) | www.festival.cz/en*

▶ ★ *Prague Book Fair:* Publishing companies from many different countries showcase their latest books. Mid-May at *Výstaviště exhibition grounds. Metro: Nádraží Holešovice (C) | svetknihy.cz*

▶ INSIDER TIP *Khamoro:* Great atmosphere and great fun – this colourful festival celebrating Roma culture takes place at the end of May. *www.khamoro.cz | in the Klub Roxy and other venues | Metro: Náměstí Republiky (B)*

▶ *Dance Prague:* Contemporary dance in June. *Divadlo Ponec, Husitská 24 a | Metro: Náměstí Republiky (B) | www.tanecpha.cz*

Classical music and jazz, cinema and literature – Prague continues to be a magnet for world-class artists and performers

▶ **Nine Gates:** A festival of Czech, German and Jewish culture with cinema, theatre and art. *First part in June, second in October | various venues | www.9bran.cz*

▶ **United Islands:** It's free and outdoors – a whole weekend at the end of June featuring world music, rock and jazz on several of the islands in the Vltava. A traditional event that attracts young people from all over Europe. *www.unitedislands. cz | on the Kampa and on Marksman's Island (Střelecký ostrov) and other locations | tram 9, 12, 20, 22: Újezd*

JULY
▶ **Folklore festival:** Music, dance and crafts around the fruit and vegetable market *(Ovocní trh)* – sometimes in July, sometimes in August. *Metro: Náměstí Republiky (B)*

SEPTEMBER
▶ **Struny podzimu** (Autumn Strings): High-quality music festival with high-profile performers (until November). It seeks to bridge the gap between classical and modern music. It attracts top names (local and international) from the world of classical music, jazz and world music. *www.strunypodzimu.cz | in the Rudolfinum and other locations | Metro: Staroměstská (A)*

OCTOBER
▶ **AghARTA Prague Jazz Festival:** Gaining in prestige as it is attracting more and more international artists. *Agharta | Železná 16 | Metro: Můstek (A, B) | www. agharta.cz*

DECEMBER
▶ **Christmas market:** Festive cheer in the magical Old Town Square, with stalls selling hot food (sausages, corn on the cob, pastries and local specialities), glühwein and traditional Czech crafts. *Staroměstské náměstí | Metro: Staroměstská (A); market also at Wenceslas Square.*

LINKS, BLOGS, APPS & MORE

▶ www.expats.cz English-language guide with jobs, chat, 24 Q&A headings and much more. Regularly updated and many postings from and for foreigners living in the Czech Republic, but tourists will also find it very useful

▶ prague.tv English-language portal with plenty of advice on where to go, which restaurant to try and also hotel recommendations. Another site for expats, so if you are thinking of staying on, consult the Jobs and Real Estate pages

▶ www.praguepost.com has all the latest news in English, including cultural reviews and previews

▶ www.360cities.net The 360° panoramic photos give an all-round view of top sights. Check out the rotating views of the Jewish Graveyard, the Kafka Statue, Charles Bridge at Night and many others

▶ www.timeout.com/prague A 'critical guide to hotels, restaurants and going out in Prague', plus lots of pages with background stories, e.g. where are the 'tank pubs' or tankovnas, where the beer comes straight from the tank

▶ There are countless other websites dedicated to meeting the needs of tourists. Here are a few of them: www.prague-guide.co.uk, www.free-prague-guide.com, www.prague-information.eu, www.pragueexperience.com

▶ www.spottedbylocals.com/prague English-language blog where expats reveal their favourite places and recent discoveries. It could be a café, a museum or a remote park

▶ www.expat-blog.com/en/directory/europe/czech-republic/prague There is a large contingent of expatriate, native English speakers in the Czech capital. Pictures, classified ads and a very lively forum. If you need specific information, then best to ask someone who lives there. Also helpful if planning to relocate

Regardless of whether you are still preparing your trip or already in Prague: these addresses will provide you with more information, videos and networks to make your holiday even more enjoyable

▶ www.euroagentur.com/en/prague-best-videos For an interesting selection of good quality videos of popular sights – from the YouTube website

▶ www.radio.cz/en/static/about-radio-prague/how-to-listen-to-radio-prague This page, produced by Prague radio service, provides information on broadcasts in English, plus a selection of podcasts

▶ Type 'The Travel Linguist Czech' into the YouTube search field and you will find a series of tutorials on how to get by in Prague with just a few simple phrases

▶ http://www.karelgott.net Intrigued by the wide appeal of Karel Gott? If so, then this website, with text also in English, will allow you, once you register, to listen to some of his hits, many of which are cover versions

▶ vimeo.com/search Sign up to Vimeo and search for Prague. View an eclectic mix of video clips ranging from a tasteful look at the city centre on a winter night to girls on skateboards

▶ TripAdvisor Want a hotel or restaurant that former patrons have rated highly? Millions of locals and travellers send comments and recommendations to this app. Available for iphones, Android phones and tablets

▶ Search the itunes website for the app that provides information on public transport connections (in Czech and English)

▶ NearestWiki GPS identifies where you are and then sends you Wikipedia pages giving background information on your current location

▶ www.couchsurfing.org Do you want to save on hotel bills? Prepared to be flexible? You don't have to sign up to find profiles. Click 'Browse People' and then enter 'Prague' in the search field. Lots of Praguers are happy to offer their gauč

▶ www.lonelyplanet.com/thorntree Travel forum with lots of practical tips. Helps newcomers and others to plan their trips to Prague

TRAVEL TIPS

Ticketcentrum | Rytířská 31 (127 F5) (ᗰ G4) and the Old Town Hall (128 B4) (ᗰ G4); Bohemia Ticket | Malé náměstí 13 (127 E5) (ᗰ G4); Ticketpro | Václavské náměstí 38 (127 F6) (ᗰ G5)

ARRIVAL

🚗 If travelling to the Czech Republic from the UK by car, then the most straightforward route is via Nuremberg in Germany, crossing the border at Waidhaus/Rozvadov. From this point follow the D5/E50 motorway to Prague via Plzeň. If you are coming from the north, i.e. Berlin, Leipzig or Dresden, the D8/E55 motorway is finished apart from a short section between Ústí nad Labem und Lovosice. Another possibility is that you arrive from Austria in the south, in which case the fastest route is the E55 Federal Highway via České Budějovice. If you are going to use motorways in the Czech Republic, then you will need to buy a windscreen sticker at the border crossing (price will depend on the duration of your stay).

🚆 If you enjoy travelling by train, then take an afternoon Eurostar from London to Brussels, then a connecting high-speed train to Cologne. From here, the 'Phoenix' City Night Line sleeper train runs to Prague and you will arrive in the city centre just after breakfast the next morning. A single journey from London costs about £90. Most trains terminate at Prague's main station (Hlavní nádraží), but some arrive at the other mainline station, Nádraží Holešovice, in the district of the same name; both have metro stations with connections to the city centre. There are three coach connections per week (Mon, Fri, Sat) between Victoria Coach Station in London and Florenc bus terminal in Prague *(www.eurolines.co.uk)*. Coach is not the most comfortable way to travel, but at £54 for a return journey, it is a cheap option and you will arrive at one of Prague's main coach stations. Please do not be tempted to carry a parcel 'for a relative'. The contents are likely to be some form of contraband.

✈ Prague's Ruzyně airport is 16km (10mi) from the city centre. Two bus routes shuttle between the city centre and the airport every 10 minutes throughout the day (fare 26Kč). No. 100 goes to the west side of the city to Zličín station on metro line B, no. 119 goes to Dejvická station on metro line A. There is also the Airport Express (AE), which costs more (50Kč), but it runs every 30 minutes straight to the main station (Hlavní nádraží). The above bus routes also run in the opposite direc-

RESPONSIBLE TRAVEL

It doesn't take a lot to be environmentally friendly whilst travelling. Don't just think about your carbon footprint whilst flying to and from your holiday destination but also about how you can protect nature and culture abroad. As a tourist it is especially important to respect nature, look out for local products, cycle instead of driving, save water and much more. If you would like to find out more about eco-tourism please visit: *www.ecotourism.org*

tion. If you would prefer to take a taxi, you are advised to use cars belonging to the AAA company. It depends on your precise destination in the city centre, but the fare will be approx. 600Kč. If you transfer into the city in a shared taxi, a white minibus belonging to the Cedaz company, you will be charged approx. 120Kč to and from Náměstí Republiky. Easyjet and British Airways serve Prague. Fares are subject to a number of variable factors, but if you have the freedom to choose your departure time and date, there are some real bargains to be had. From the United States, Delta Air Lines operates direct flights to Prague.

BANKS & MONEY

If you are going to change money in a bank, you will need your passport or an identity card. The charges at bureaux de change are usually much higher than in banks. You will find plenty of cash machines in the city centre. Almost all hotels, shops and restaurants accept credit cards; many will also take euros.
LOST CREDIT CARDS (EMERGENCY NOS.)
American Express tel. 2 22 80 02 22 | Visa tel. 2 72 77 11 11 | Diners Club tel. 2 67 19 74 50

CONSULATES & EMBASSIES

UK EMBASSY
Thunovska 14 | 118 00 Prague 1 | tel. 2 57 40 21 11 | http://ukinczechrepublic. fco.gov.uk/en/ | info@britain.cz

US EMBASSY
Tržiště 15 | 118 01 Praha 1 - Malá Strana | tel. 2 57 02 20 00 | http://prague.usembassy.gov | ACSPrg@state.gov

BUDGETING

Espresso	£1.20/2.00US$
	for a cup
Ice-cream	£0.80/1.20US$
	for a scoop
Beer	£1.20/2.00US$
	for one glass (0.5 l)
Metro:	£0.80/1.20US$
	for a single ticket
Snack	£1.60/2.50US$
	for a small sausage

CUSTOMS

There are no longer customs controls at the borders, but the officials are entitled to carry out random checks. Every adult may take the following items with them duty-free on entry from the Czech Republic: 800 cigarettes or 400 cigarillos or 200 cigars or 1 kg tobacco, plus 110 l beer, 90 l wine, 10 l spirits and medications for personal use. There is also a limit on the import of fuel. As well as a full tank of fuel, you may also carry a 20-litre reserve canister.

DISCOUNTED ADMISSION TICKETS

The Prague Information Service or PIS sells a special tourist ticket for 400Kč. Called the *Ten Prague Monuments Pass*, it offers a significant discount. The pass will give you admission, over a period of three days, to several towers: the observation tower on Petřín Hill, the Powder Tower, the towers at the Charles Bridge, and the ones on the Old Town Hall and on the Church of St Nicholas in the Lesser Town. It also grants admission to the Mirror Mazeon on Petřín Hill. You can buy the pass at any of the above sights.

The Prague Card also offers discounts to many attractions, too many for most tourists on short breaks. As well as a free bus tour of the city, it will open the door to over 40 museums and monuments, including the castle and the Old Town Hall, the National Gallery, the Jewish Town and the Mirror Maze on Petřín Hill. For some attractions, it entitles the holder only to a price reduction. You can buy a Prague Card in branches of the PIS and also online at *www.praguecitycard.com*. A card can be valid for two days *(790Kč)*, three days *(980Kč)* or four days *(1200Kč)*.

DRIVING

Drink-driving is strictly illegal in the Czech Republic. In built-up areas the maximum speed is 50 kmph, outside built-up areas 90 kmph, on motorways 130 kmph. Daytime running lights are compulsory throughout the year.

On-road parking in central Prague can be very difficult. The only available spaces are almost always reserved for residents. If you park illegally, be prepared for a fine in the region of 5,000Kč. An alternative to the expensive underground or multi-storey car parks (approx. 1,000Kč/24hrs) are the CCTV-monitored parking lots (approx. 50Kč/per hour). There is a multi-story car park near Náměstí Jana Palacha, entrance from Dvořákovo nábřeží. By far the best option when driving into Prague is 'Park and Ride'. There are car parks at these stations: Skalka, Zličín, Nové Butovice, Radlická, Opatov, Rajská zahrada, Černý Most and Nádraží Holešovice.

EMERGENCY SERVICES

Central emergency no. *tel.* 112; fire *tel.* 150; police *tel.* 158; roadside assistance *tel.* 12 30; ambulance *tel.* 155

EVENTS CALENDAR

The English-language 'Prague Post' is published every Thursday and includes a complete 'what's on' listing. Promotional magazines are given away in many pubs, bars and restaurants and in PIS branches. The free magazine *Houser* provides an excellent summary of what's happening.

GUIDED TOURS

The Prague Information Service will supply official city guides and organise sightseeing tours. Numerous travel agencies in the city offer almost identical excursions. It is well worth doing a quick price comparison. The main providers are Prague Tourist Centre *(corner of Rytířská/Na můstku* (128 C5) *(𝄐 G4) | tel. 2 24 21 22 09)* and Martin Tour *(Štěpánská 61* (133 A2) *(𝄐 G5) | tel. 2 24 21 24 73)* and also Sandeman's New Europe Prague (bookable only over the internet at www.newpraguetours.com). Posters dotted around the city centre (in English) advertise alternative sightseeing tours. The meeting place is usually the Powder Tower by Náměstí Republiky or the Old Town Square. Another way of seeing the city is from the river. Tickets for river trips can be purchased on the quayside *(Rašínovo nábřeží* (127 F5) *(𝄐 F6)* or *Dvořákovo nábřeží* (128 B3) *(𝄐 F3))* or from *Čedok (Na příkopě 18* (127 F5) *(𝄐 G4) | tel. 2 21 44 72 42)*.

HEALTH

A first-aid service is available for emergencies and treatment is usually free of charge.
– *Emergency pharmacy service: Lékárna | Palackého 5* (132 A2) *(𝄐 G5) | tel. 2 24 94 69 82*
– *Hospital: Hospital Na Homolce (foreign language service) | Roentgenova 2* (0) *(𝄐 0) | tel. 2 57 27 11 11 | from Anděl*

metro station (line B) then bus no. 167 as for as the terminus
– Emergency dental service: Spálená 12 (131 E2) (*G5*) | tel. 2 22 92 42 68

IMMIGRATION

The Czech Republic is a member of the Schengen group of countries and there are no passport controls, if arriving from all neighbouring EU countries. Citizens of the EU and the USA need a full passport to enter the country. UK citizens can stay for 180 days without a visa. All other EU and US citizens can stay for up to 90 days. But you must still keep your passport with you at all times.

INFORMATION

CZECH TOURIST AUTHORITY
– 13 Harley Street | London W1G 9QG UK | tel. 0207 63 10 427 | info-uk@czechtourism.com
– 1109 Madison Avenue | New York, N. Y. 10028 | USA | tel. 0212 2 88 08 30 | info-usa@czechtourism.com
– Online: www.czechtourism.com

INFORMATION IN PRAGUE

PIS (PRAGUE INFORMATION SERVICE)
– Old Town Hall | Staroměstské náměstí 1 (127 E5) (*G4*) | daily 9am–8pm
– Rytířská 31 (127 F5) (*G4*) | Mon–Fri 9am–7pm
– Main station| Wilsonova 8 (129 D5) (f H4) | Mon–Sat 10am–6pm
– Airport | Terminal 2 (0) (*O*) | daily 8am–8pm
– Tel. 2 21 71 44 44

INTERNET CAFÉS

There are plenty of computer terminals available in Prague's internet cafés, e.g. in Káva Káva Káva | Národní 37 (128 B5) (*G4*), in Spika | Dlážděná 4

(129 D4) (*H4*), Bohemia Bagel | Masná 2 (128 C4) (*G3*) and in The Globe | Pštrossova 6 (131 E2) (*F5*).

LOST & FOUND

Karolíny Světlé 5 (128 B5) (*F4*) | tel. 2 24 23 50 85 | Metro: Národní třída (B)

PHONE & MOBILE PHONE

All numbers, landline and mobile, in the Czech Republic have nine digits. The country code, 00 420, is not followed by an area code, as this is part of the landline number. Mobile numbers do not begin with a 0, but with a 6 or a 7. If you have any enquiries, call 1180. Use these country codes, if dialling home: UK (0044) or USA (001).

CURRENCY CONVERTER

£	Kč	Kč	£
1	32	1	0.03
3	96	3	0.09
5	160	5	0.15
13	420	13	0.40
40	1,290	40	1.24
75	2,415	75	2.30
120	3,870	120	3.72
250	8,000	250	7.75
500	16,100	500	15.50

$	Kč	Kč	$
1	20.60	1	0.05
3	62	3	0.15
5	103	5	0.24
13	267	13	0.63
40	825	40	1.94
75	1,545	75	3.65
120	2,470	120	5.80
250	5,150	250	12
500	10,300	500	24

For current exchange rates see www.xe.com

Telephone cards *(telefonní karta)* may be purchased from post offices *(pošta)* and in kiosks and tobacconists *(trafika)*. O2 Telefónica's Xcall is the cheapest way to call home. You use the 970 prefix, e.g. to call the UK, dial 970 00 44. You will only pay approx 4Kč per minute. However, this applies only to calls from landlines. If you call from a phone box, you will pay about 15Kč per minute. To charge your mobile phone, you will need an adapter for continental sockets.

POST

General post office: *Jindřišská 14* **(132 B1)** *(◻ G4)* | tel. 2 21 13 11 11 | Metro: Můstek *(A, B)* Letters and postcards to elsewhere in Europe cost 20Kč.

PRICES & CURRENCY

Coins are denominated at 1, 2, 5, 10, 20 and 50Kč, banknotes at 100, 200, 500, 1000, 2000 and 5000Kč.

Prague is still a fairly cheap place for western tourists, but do not underestimate the entrepreneurial skills of the business community in the city centre. You will pay 'big city' prices in the restaurants, hotels and shops there. Ticket prices for cultural events, on the other hand, are very reasonable. Cinema tickets cost about 170Kč, museums between 70 and 200Kč, for a good theatre performance or a concert reckon on about 700Kč. Admission to discos and clubs starts at 150Kč, but if a well-known DJ or an international star is performing, a ticket could cost up to 400Kč.

PUBLIC TRANSPORT

The same *jízdenky* (tickets) can be used on all of the city's public transport services, and that includes tram, metro and

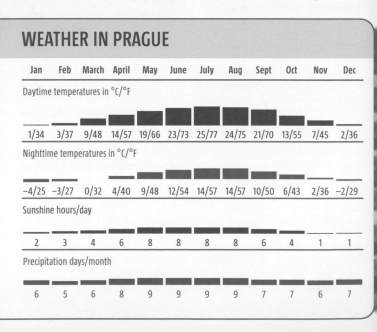

WEATHER IN PRAGUE

	Jan	Feb	March	April	May	June	July	Aug	Sept	Oct	Nov	Dec
Daytime temperatures in °C/°F												
	1/34	3/37	9/48	14/57	19/66	23/73	25/77	24/75	21/70	13/55	7/45	2/36
Nighttime temperatures in °C/°F												
	−4/25	−3/27	0/32	4/40	9/48	12/54	14/57	14/57	10/50	6/43	2/36	−2/29
Sunshine hours/day												
	2	3	4	6	8	8	8	8	6	4	1	1
Precipitation days/month												
	6	5	6	8	9	9	9	9	7	7	6	7

bus. A 24Kč ticket is valid for journey up to 30 mins, a 32Kč ticket for 90 mins. You can change as many times as you like within that time. Children aged between ten and 15 years of age, as well as senior citizens from the age of 65, pay half. Children younger than ten travel free of charge. If you have a dog or a large piece of luggage, then you must buy a 16Kč ticket. Single tickets are available from machines (if there are any) at the stops or at pavement kiosks; travel passes at the two *airport terminals* or *at Muzeum, and Anděl metro stations: 24-hour ticket 110Kč, 72-hour ticket 310Kč.*

Travellers caught without a valid ticket can expect a fine of between 400 and 1000Kč. There are no barriers, but inspectors make frequent random checks. The *tramvaj* (tram) service extends into the suburbs. At night, the main routes are covered by the 51–58 lines, the central transfer station being *Lazarská*. The metro runs between 5am and midnight.

TAXI

Despite the new tariff introduced in 2007, whereby meters show a standard charge of 28Kč per km, some drivers demand extortionate prices. As a general rule, you can rely on the services offered by the two main taxi companies, *AAA (tel. 140 14, tel. 2 22 33 32 22)* and *City-Taxi (tel. 2 57 25 72 57)*. Visitors will gain some reassurance from the 'Fair Place' notices, posted at supervised taxi ranks in central locations in the city. Listed here are guide prices for some of the most popular destinations. As a general rule, always ask for the taximeter to be switched on. That is compulsory. If you are going to negotiate a price, you will usually pay over the odds. The receipt must be printed out from the taximeter. A hand-written receipt is not valid. The basic fare for a journey is 40Kč and waiting times are charged at up to 6Kč per minute. If you think you have been overcharged, then by all means complain at the Town Hall *(Mariánské náměstí 2)*. It is probably unlikely that you will be compensated for your loss, but the city authorities need to know that malpractices are still taking place. For many years, the taxi business has been under the spotlight and attempts to rein in rogue traders are ongoing.

Remember that drinking even a tiny amount of alcohol and then driving is illegal. If you can't resist a drink and don't want to abandon your car, then you can always call on the **INSIDER TIP** 'Blue Angel' service *(Modrý anděl | tel. 7 37 22 23 33)*. They will drive you and your own car home. Pick-up guaranteed in 20 minutes or less.

TOURIST RIP-OFFS

Prague is no crime capital. But as in other big cities, fraudsters abound. There are restaurants where a cover charge, a seemingly complimentary brandy or a charge for live music are unexpectedly added to the bill. If you are dissatisfied with the charges, ask to speak to the manager. In most cases, he will not want to be involved in a potentially embarrassing scene. As a general rule, make sure you receive a clear, itemised receipt. If you consider yourself to be the victim of a crime, call the police. They do not like swindlers.

Petty criminals will take advantage of unwary tourists, so take great care. Pickpockets ride the metro disguised as tourists; sometimes they emerge from behind the panels showing maps of the city, others wait in side streets and pretend to be plainclothes policemen and then proceed to confiscate 'counterfeit banknotes' from your wallet. These gangs can be ruthless and violent.

If you are dissatisfied with any Czech officials you encounter, please contact the *British Embassy on 2 57 40 21 11 or the US Embassy on 257 022 000.*

NOTES

FOR YOUR NEXT HOLIDAY ...

MARCO POLO TRAVEL GUIDES

ALGARVE
AMSTERDAM
ATHENS
AUSTRALIA
BANGKOK
BARCELONA
BERLIN
BRUSSELS
BUDAPEST
CALIFORNIA
CAMBODIA
CAPE TOWN
  WINE LANDS,
  GARDEN ROUTE
CHINA
COLOGNE
COPENHAGEN
CORFU
COSTA BLANCA
  VALENCIA
COSTA DEL SOL
  GRANADA
CRETE
CUBA

CYPRUS
  NORTH AND
  SOUTH
DUBAI
DUBLIN
DUBROVNIK &
  DALMATIAN COAST
EDINBURGH
EGYPT
FINLAND
FLORENCE
FLORIDA
FRENCH RIVIERA
  NICE, CANNES &
  MONACO
FUERTEVENTURA
GRAN CANARIA
HONG KONG
  MACAU
ICELAND
IRELAND
ISRAEL
ISTANBUL
JORDAN

KOS
KRAKOW
LAKE GARDA
LANZAROTE
LAS VEGAS
LISBON
LONDON
LOS ANGELES
MADEIRA
  PORTO SANTO
MADRID
MALLORCA
MALTA
  GOZO
MOROCCO
MUNICH
NEW YORK
NEW ZEALAND
NORWAY
OSLO
PARIS

PRAGUE
RHODES
ROME
SAN FRANCISCO
SARDINIA
SHANGHAI
SICILY
SOUTH AFRICA
STOCKHOLM
TENERIFE
THAILAND
TURKEY
TURKEY
  SOUTH COAST
TUSCANY
UNITED ARAB
  EMIRATES
VENICE
VIENNA
VIETNAM

- PACKED WITH INSIDER TIPS
- BEST WALKS AND TOURS
- FULL-COLOUR PULL-OUT MAP
  AND STREET ATLAS

USEFUL PHRASES CZECH

PRONUNCIATION

To simplify the pronunciation:
In spite of only a few vowels, a lot of háčky (hooks) and čárky (acute accents), the pronunciation is actually not all that difficult. Usually, the first syllable is stressed.

c like ts	ě like ye	š like sch
č as in choke	ň like nye	ť like tye
ch like k	ř like rsch	z like s
ď like dj	s like ss	ž like dz

IN BRIEF

Yes/No	Ano ['ahno]/Ne [nay]
Please	Prosím ['prossimm]
Thank you	Děkuji ['jekui]
You're welcome	Rádo se stalo ['rahdo se 'stalo]
Could you help me please?	Prosím vás, můžete mi pomoci? ['prossimm vas 'musheteh mi 'pomotsi]
Help!	Pomoc! ['pomots]
I would like to .../	Chtěl/-a bych ... ['shtell /-a bich]
Have you got ...?	Máte ...? ['mahteh]
How much is it?	Kolik to stojí? ['kolik to 'stoyee]
What time is it?	Kolik je hodin? ['kolik yay 'hodeen]
Excuse me, please!	Promiňte! ['promintyeh]
Pardon?	Prosím? ['prossimm]
I don't understand you	Nerozumím vám/ti ['nerohsumeem varm/tyi]

GREETINGS, FAREWELL

Good morning!	Dobré jitro! ['dobray 'yutro]
Good afternoon!	Dobrý den! ['dobray 'den]
Good evening!	Dobrý večer! ['dobray 'vetchair]
Hello!	Ahoj! [a'hoi]
What's your name, please?	Jaké je vaše jméno, prosím? ['yakay yay 'vasha 'mayno 'prossimm]
My name is ...	Jmenuji se ... ['menuyi say]
I'm from ...	Jsem z ... ['sem se]

Mluvíš Česky?

'Do you speak Czech?' This guide will help you to say the basic words and phrases in Czech

How do you do?	Jak se máte/máš? ['yek se 'mahtay/'maash]
Thank you for asking. And you?	Děkuji. A vy/ty? ['jekui a 'vee/tee]
Goodbye!	Na shledanou! ['na skledanoo]
See you!	Ahoj! [a'hoi]

TRAVEL

Information

Pardon, where can I find ...?	Prosím vás, kde je ...? ['prossimm 'vass gde jey]
train station	nádraží ['nadrashi]
track/platform	kolej ['kolay]
airport	letiště ['letyishtyay]
stop	zastávka ['sastahfka]
taxi/cab stand	stanoviště taxíků ['stonovistyay 'taxikoo]
Where can I buy a ticket?	Kde si můžu koupit lístek? ['gde si 'mooshoo 'koopit 'listek]
How far is it?	Jak je to daleko? ['yak yey to 'daleko]
Cross ...	Přejděte ... ['pshaydyaitay]
... the bridge	... přes most ['psheshmosst]
... the square	... přes náměstí ['pshesnaamestyi]
... the road	... přes ulici ['pshes oolitsi]
open	otevřený ['otevshenyi]
closed	zavřeno ['savresheno]
entrance	vchod ['fhot]
exit	východ ['fshot]
Keep going straight ahead ...	Pořád rovně až ... ['porshat 'rovnye ash]
Then turn left/right	Potom odbočte (zahněte) do leva/do prava ['potom 'odbotshte ('sahnyehte) 'dolava/'doprava]

petrol/gas station

I would like ... litres	Chtěl/-a bych ... litrů ['shtyel/-a bich ... litroo]
... premium gas	... benzínu super ['benzinoo 'super]
... diesel	... nafty ['nafty]
Full, please	Plnou (nádrž) prosím ['plnoo ('nahdrsch) 'prossimm]

Accident

There has been an accident!	Stala se nehoda! ['stalaa sey 'neyhoda]
Please call ... quickly	Zavolejte prosím rychle ... ['savoleytay 'prossimm 'hrichley]
... an ambulance	... sanitku ['sanitkoo]
... the police	... policii ['politsiyi]
... the fire brigade	... požárníky ['posharniki]
It was my/your fault	Byla to moje/vaše vina ['beela to 'moyey/'vashey veena]
Please give me your name and address	Napište mi prosím své jméno a adresu ['napishtey mi 'prossimm svey 'meyno a 'adressoo]
Many thanks for your help	Děkuji vám za pomoc ['djekui vem 'sapomots]

FOOD & DRINK

Where is there a good restaurant here?	Kde je tady nějaká dobrá restaurace? ['gde ye 'tadi 'nyeyakaa 'dobra 'restauratsey?]
I'd like ...	Dal/-a bych si ... ['dal/-a bish si]
Cheers!	Na vaše zdraví! ['navasha 'sdravee]
I didn't order that	To jsem si neobjednal/-a ['to sem si 'neyobyednal/-a]
May I have the bill, please?	Platit prosím ['platyeet 'prossimm]
Did you like it?	Chutnalo vám? ['chutnalo vamm]
It was excellent	Bylo to výborné ['bilo to 'viborney]

ACCOMMODATION

Can you recommend ... please?	Můžete mi prosím doporučit ... ['muhshetey mi 'prossimm 'doporutshit]
... a good hotel ...	... nějaký dobrý hotel? ['nyehak 'dobree 'hotel]
... a pension ...	... penzión? ['pänsijon]
Do you have any rooms left?	Máte ještě volné pokoje? ['mahtay 'yestyay 'volnay 'pokoyeh]
single room	Jednolůžkový ['yedno'looshkovee]
double room	Dvoulůžkový ['dvoo'looshkovee]
shower/sit-down bath	se sprchou/s koupelnou ['se sprookoo /'skoupelnoo]
for one night	na jednu noc ['nayednoo 'nots]
for one week	na týden ['nateeden]
How much is this room including breakfast?	Kolik stojí pokoj se snídaní? ['kolik 'stoyee 'pokoy 'se snidane]

HEALTH

Can you recommend a good doctor?	Můžete mi doporučit nějakého dobrého lékaře? ['moshetey mi 'doporut-shit 'nyeyyakeho 'dobreyho 'lekarsha]
I have pain here	Mám bolesti tady ['mamm 'bolesti 'tadi]
I have a temperature	Mám horečku ['mamm 'heretshku]

BANKS & MONEY

I would like to exchange money	Chtěl/-a bych vyměnit peníze ['shtell/-a bish vimyenyit penyishe]
Please, where can I find ...	Kde je tady ... ['gde yay 'tadi]
... a bank?	... banka? ['banka]
... an ATM?	... peněžní automat? ['penyishnyeh 'automat]

POST

How much do you put on ...	Kolik se dává ['colic se 'davah]
... a letter	... na dopis ['nadopis]
... a postcard	... na lístek ['nalistek]

NUMBERS

0	nula ['nuala]	18	osmnáct ['ossumnaatst]
1	jeden (m)/jedna (f) [yayden/'yedna]	19	devatenáct ['devatenaatst]
2	dva (m) ['dva], dvě (f) ['dvy-ey]	20	dvacet [dvatset]
3	tři ['trshi]	21	dvacet jedna ['dvatset 'yedna]
4	čtyři ['shtirshi]	30	třicet ['chitset]
5	pět ['pyet]	40	čtyřicet ['chtirchitset]
6	šest [shest]	50	padesát ['padessaht]
7	sedm ['sedumm]	60	šedesát [shedessaht]
8	osm ['ossumm]	70	sedmdesát ['sedumdessaht]
9	devět ['devyet]	80	osmdesát ['ossummdessaht]
10	deset ['desset]	90	devadesát ['devahdesaht]
11	jedenáct ['yeydenahtst]	100	sto ['sto]
12	dvanáct ['dvanahtst]	200	dvě stě ['dvye 'stye]
13	třináct ['tshinahtst]	300	tři sta ['chi 'stya]
14	čtrnáct ['shtrnahtst]	1000	tisíc ['tisseets]
15	patnáct ['patnahtst]	2000	dva tisíce ['dva 'tissetsya]
16	šestnáct ['shestnahtst]	½	půl [pool]
17	sedmnáct ['sedummnahtst]	¼	čtvrt [(t)shtvert]

STREET ATLAS

The green line ▭ **indicates the Walking tours (p. 100–105)**

All tours are also marked on the pull-out map

Photo: the Vltava River in Prague

Exploring Prague

The map on the back cover shows how the area has been sub-divided

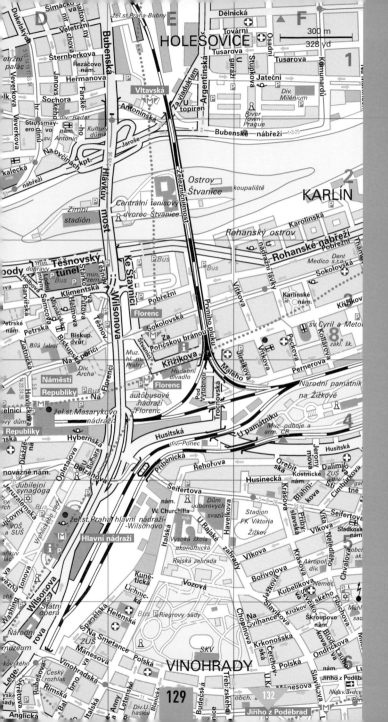

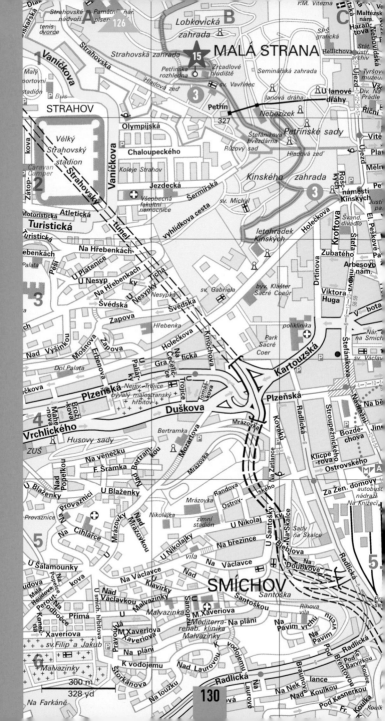

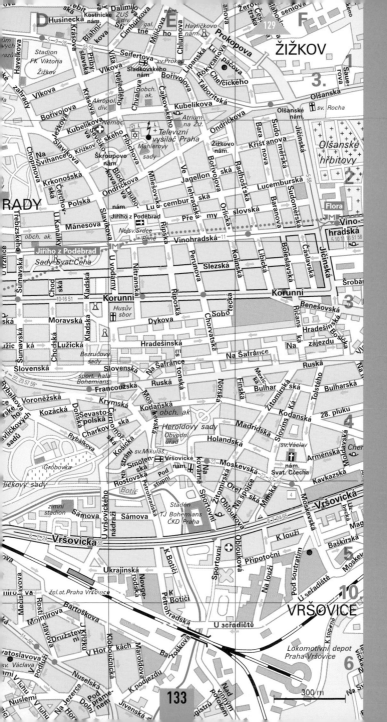

ŽIŽKOV

VINOHRADY

VRŠOVICE

133

300 m

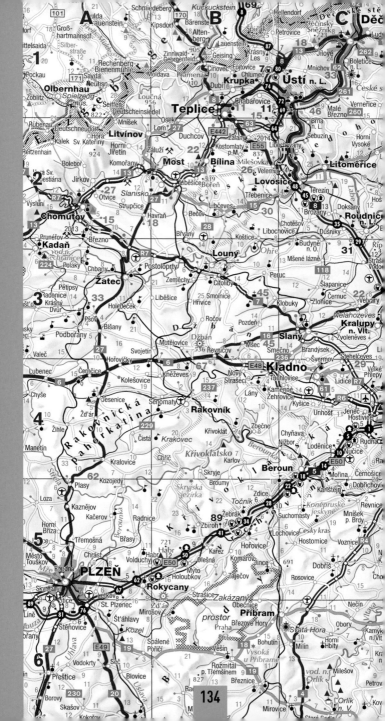

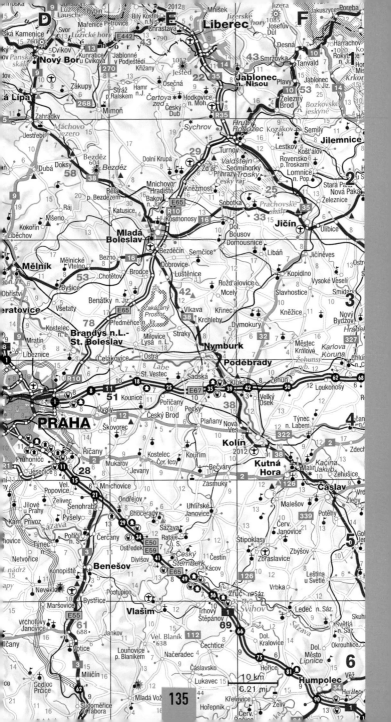

This index lists a selection of the streets and squares shown on the street atlas

1...9
5. května **132/B6**
17. listopadu **128/B3-B4**
28. pluku **133/F4**
28. října **128/C5**

A
Albertov **132/A5-B4**
Alšovo nábřeží **128/A4-B4**
Americká **132/C3-C4**
Anenská **128/B5**
Anežská **128/C3**
Anglická **132/B3**
Anny Letenské **132/C2-C3**
Antonínska **129/E1-E2**
Apolinářská **132/A4-B4**
Arbesovo náměstí **130/C3**
Argentinska **129/E1**
Arménská **133/F4**

B
Bachmačské náměstí **126/B2**
Badeniho **127/D2-D3**
Balbínova **129/D6**
Banskobystrická **126/A2**
Baranova **133/F2**
Bartolomějská **128/B5**
Bartoškova **133/D5-E6**
Barvířská **129/D3**
Bělehradská **132/B3-C5**
Belgicka **132/C3-C4**
Benátská **131/E4-F4**
Benediktská **128/C3-C4**
Benešovská **133/F3**
Betlémská **128/A5-B5**
Betlémské náměstí **128/B5**
Bieblova **130/B5-C5**
Bílkova **128/B3**
Biskupská **129/D3**
Blahnikova **129/F5**
Blanická **132/C2-C3**
Blodkova **133/E2**
Boleslavova **132/C6**
Boleslavská **133/F2-F3**
Bolzanova **129/D4**
Bořivojova **133/D1-E2**
Botičská **131/E4**
Bozděchova **130/C4**
Boženy Němcové **132/B4**
Braunova **130/C6**
Břehová **128/B3**
Brožíkova **130/A4**
Bruselská **132/C4**
Brusnice **126/A3-B4**
Bubenečska **126/C1-C2**
Bubenská **129/D1-E1**
Bubenské nábřeží **129/E2-F2**
Budečská **133/D2-D3**
Bulharská **133/F4**
Buštéhradská **126/A2-A3**
Buzulucká **126/B2**

C
Celakovského sady **129/D6**
Celetná **128/C4**
Cihelná **127/D4**
Cimburkova **129/F4-F5**
Ctiborova **132/C5**
Ctiradova **133/D5**

Č
Čajkovského **133/E1-E2**
Čáslavská **133/F3**
Čechova **128/B1**
Čechův most **128/B3**
Čerchovská **133/D2**
Čermákova **132/C4-133/D4**
Černá **128/B6**
Černínská **126/A4**
Černomořská **133/E4**
Českomalínská **126/C1**
Československé armády **126/B2-C2**
Čestmírova **133/D5**
Číklova **132/B6**

D
Dalimilova **129/F4**
Dejvická **126/B2-C2**
Dělnická **129/E1-F1**
Dělostřelecká **126/A3**
Divadelní **128/A5**
Dittrichova **131/E3**
Dlážděná **129/D4**
Dlouhá **128/B4-C3**
Dobrovského **128/C1-C2**
Donská **133/D4**
dr. Zikmunda Wintra **126/C1**
Dražického náměstí **126/C4-127/D4**
Dřevná **131/D4-E4**
Drtinova **130/C3**
Družstevni **133/D6**
Dukelských hrdinů **129/D1-D2**
Duškova **130/B4**
Dušní **128/B3**
Dvořákovo nábřeží **128/B3-C3**
Dykova **133/E3**

E
Eliášova **126/C1-C2**
Elišky Krásnohorské **128/B3**
Elišky Peškové **130/C2-C3**
Erbenova **130/A3-A4**
Estonská **133/E3-E4**
Evropská **126/A2**

F
Farského **129/D1-D2**
Fibichova **133/E2**
Finská **133/F4**
Flemingovo náměstí **126/A1**
Francouzská **132/C3-133/E4**
Františka Křížka **129/D1-D2**
Fričova **132/C5**
Fügnerovo náměstí **132/B4**

G
Generála Píky **126/A2-B2**
Gerstnerova **128/C1**
Gogolova **127/D3**
Gorazdova **131/E3**
Grafická **130/A4-B3**
Gymnasijní **126/A2**

H
Hálkova **131/F3**
Harantova **126/C5**
Haškova **128/C1**
Haštalská **128/C3**

Haštalske náměstí **128/C3**
Havanská **128/B1**
Havelkova **129/E5**
Havelská **128/B5**
Havelská ulička **128/C3**
Havířská **128/C5**
Havlíčkova **129/D4**
Havlíčkovo náměstí **133/E1**
Helénská **129/E6**
Hellichova **126/C5**
Helmova **129/D3**
Heřmanova **128/C1-129/D1**
Hlávkův most **129/D2-E2**
Hlavova **131/F5**
Holandská **133/E4-F4**
Holbova **129/D3**
Holečkova **130/A4-C2**
Hořejší nábřeží **131/D4-D5**
Horská **132/A5-B5**
Hradčanské náměstí **126/B4**
Hradební **128/C3**
Hradešínská **133/E3-F3**
Hroznova **127/D4**
Husinecká **129/F4-F5**
Husitská **129/E4-F4**
Husova **128/B4-B5**
Hybernská **129/D4**

Ch
Chaloupeckého **130/A2-B2**
Charkovská **133/D4-E4**
Charlese de Gaulla **126/B1**
Charvátova **128/B5-C5**
Chelčického **133/E1-F1**
Chlumova **133/E1**
Chodská **133/D2-D3**
Chopinova **129/F6**
Chorvatská **133/E3**
Chotkova **126/C3-127/D3**
Chvalova **133/E1**

I
Ibsenova **132/C3**
Italská **132/C1-C3**

J
Jáchymova **128/B4**
Jagellonská **133/E2**
Jakubská **128/C4**
Jana Masaryka **132/C4**
Jana Zajíce **128/B1**
Janáčkovo nábřeží **131/D2-D4**
Janovského **129/D1**
Jaromírova **132/B5**
Jaselská **126/C2**
Jateční **129/F1**
Ječná **131/E3-F3**
Jelení **126/A3**
Jeronymova **129/F4**
Jeruzalémská **129/D5**
Jezdecká **130/A2-B2**
Ježkova **133/D1-D2**
Jičínská **133/F2-F3**
Jilemnického **126/C2**
Jilská **128/B4-B5**
Jindřicha Plachty **130/C4-131/D4**
Jindřišská **128/C5-129/D5**
Jiráskovo náměstí **131/D3**
Jiráskův most **131/D3**
Jirečkova **128/C1**

STREET INDEX

Jirsikova **129/F4**
Josefská **126/C4**
Jugoslávská **132/B3-C3**
Jugoslávských partyzánů **126/B1**
Jungmannova **128/C5-C6**
Jungmannovo náměstí **128/C5**

K
K Botiči **133/E5**
K Brusce **126/C2-C3**
K louži **133/F5**
K podjezou **133/E6**
K vodojemu **130/A6-B6**
Kafkova **126/A2-B2**
Kamenická **128/C1-C2**
Kamzíková **128/C4**
Kanovnická **126/B4**
Kaprova **128/B4**
Karlínské náměstí **129/F3**
Karlova **128/B4**
Karlovo náměstí **131/E3**
Karlův most **127/D5**
Karmelitska **126/C5**
Karolíny **128/A5-B5**
Kartouzská **130/B4-C3**
Kateřinská **132/A3**
Kavkazská **133/F4**
Ke Hradu **126/B4**
Ke Karlovu **132/A3-B4**
Ke Koulce **130/C6**
Ke Stranici **129/E3**
Keplerova **126/A4**
Kladská **133/D3**
Klárov **126/D4**
Klášterská **128/C3**
Klimentská **128/C3-129/D3**
Kloboučnická **133/E6**
Kmochova **130/B3-B4**
Kodaňská **133/E4-F3**
Kolejni **126/A1**
Kolinská **133/E3-F3**
Kollárova **129/F3**
Kommunardů **129/F1**
Konviktská **128/B5**
Koperníkova **132/C4-133/D4**
Kořenského **130/C3-131/D3**
Korunni **132/C3-133/F3**
Korunovační **128/B1**
Kosárkovo nábřeží **128/A3-A4**
Košická **133/E4**
Kostelní **128/C2-129/D2**
Kostnicke náměstí **129/F4**
Koubkova **132/B4**
Kováků **130/B4-C5**
Kozácká **133/D4**
Kozí **128/B3-C4**
Kožná **128/B4**
Krakovská **128/C6**
Králodvorská **128/C4**
Krásova **129/F5**
Křemencova **128/B6**
Křesomyslova **132/B5-C5**
Křišt'anova **133/F2**
Křižíkova **129/E4-F3**
Křižovnická **128/B4**
Křižovnické náměstí **128/A4-A5**
Křižovského **133/D2-E2**
Krkonošská **133/D2**
Krocinova **128/A5-B5**
Kroftova **130/C2-C3**
Krokova **131/F6**
Krymská **133/D4-E4**
Kubelikova **133/D2-E1**

Kunětická **129/E5**
Kyjevská **126/B2**

L
Lannova **128/C3-129/D3**
Laubova **133/E2**
Lazarská **128/B6**
Legerova **132/B2-B4**
Letenská **126/C4-127/D4**
Letenské náměstí **128/C1**
Letohradská **128/C2-129/D2**
Libická **133/F3**
Libušina **131/D5-E5**
Lichnická **129/E5**
Lidická **130/C4-131/D4**
Liliová **128/B4-B5**
Lipanská **133/E1**
Lípová **131/F3**
Lodní mlýny **129/D3**
Londýnská **132/B3-C4**
Loretánská **126/A4-B4**
Lounských **132/B3-B4**
Lublaňská **132/B3-B4**
Lucemburská **133/E2-F2**
Lumírova **132/A6**
Lupačova **133/E1-F1**
Lužická **133/D3**

M
Máchova **132/C4-133/D4**
Madridská **133/E4-F4**
Magdalény Rettigové **128/B6**
Maiselova **128/B4**
Malá **12G/A2**
Malá Štěpánská **131/F3**
Malá Štupartská **128/C4**
Malátova **130/C2-131/D2**
Malé náměstí **128/B4**
Malého **129/E4-F4**
Maliřská **128/C1**
Malostranské nábřeží **127/D6**
Malostranské náměstí **126/C4**
Maltézské náměstí **126/C5**
Mánesova **129/E6-F6**
Mánesův most **128/A4**
Maříkova **126/C2**
Mariánské hradby **126/B3-C3**
Mariánské náměstí **128/B4**
Maroldova **133/E6**
Masarykovo nábřeží **128/A6**
Masná **128/C4**
Matoušova **130/C3-131/D3**
Mečislavova **133/D5-D6**
Melantrichova **128/B4-B5**
Mělnická **126/C6**
Mezibranská **128/C6-129/D6**
Michalská **128/B4-B5**
Mickiewiczova **126/C3-127/D3**
Mikovcova **132/B3**
Mikulandská **128/B5-B6**
Milady Horákové **126/A3-128/C1**
Milešovská **133/E2**
Milíčova **131/E1**
Minská **133/F5**
Mišenská **126/C4-127/D4**
Myslbekova **126/A4**
Mlynářská **129/D3**
Mojmírova **133/D6**
Moldavská **133/F4**
Moravská **132/C3-133/D3**
Moskevská **133/E4-F5**
Mošnova **130/A3-A4**

most Legií **127/D6**
Mostecká **126/C4-C5**
Mozartova **130/B4**
Mrázovka **130/B4**
Muchova **126/C2**
Muzejni **128/C1**
Myslíkova **128/B6**

N
N a baště svatého Jiří **126/C3**
N a baště svatého Ludmily
  126/C3-127/D3
N a baště svatého Tomáše **127/D3**
N a bělidle **130/C4-131/D4**
Na bojišti **132/B3**
N a březince **130/B5**
N a Bučance **131/F6**
Na čečeličce **130/B3-B4**
Na Celné **131/D4**
Na Cihlářce **130/A5**
N a Děkance **131/E4-E5**
Na Florenci **129/D3-E3**
Na Folimance **132/B5-C5**
Na Františku **128/C3**
N a hrádku **131/E4**
N a Hřebenkách **130/A3**
Na hrobci **131/E5**
Na hutích **126/B2**
Na Kampě **127/D5**
Na Kleovce **130/B4**
Na kovárně **133/E4**
Na Kozačce **130/B4**
N a květnici **132/C6-133/D6**
Na Laurové **130/B6**
Na louži **133/F5**
Na Moráni **131/E3**
N a můstku **128/C5**
Na Neklance **130/B6-C6**
Na Opyši **126/C3-127/D3**
N a Ořechovce **126/A3**
Na ostrůvku **132/C5**
N a ovčinách **129/D2**
Na Pankráci **132/A6-B6**
Na Perštýne **128/B5**
N a pláni **130/A6-B6**
N a poříčí **128/C4-129/D3**
N a příkopě **128/C4-C5**
Na Provaznici **130/A5**
Na Rybníčku **131/F3**
N a Šafrance **133/E4-F3**
Na Šejcharu **127/D2**
Na Skalce **130/B4**
Na Slovanech **131/E4**
Na slupi **131/E4-F5**
Na Smetance **129/D6-E6**
Na spojce **133/E5-F4**
Na stráni **133/E4**
Na Švihance **133/D2**
N a Václavce **130/A5-B5**
Na valech **133/B3-127/D2**
Na Valentince **131/D5**
N a Věnečku **130/A4**
N a Vítězné pláni **132/B6-C6**
N a výšinách **128/D1**
N a výtoni **131/E4-E5**
N a zájezdu **133/F3**
N a Zámecke **132/C5**
Na Zatlance **130/B4**
N a Zátorce **127/D1-D2**
Na zbořenci **128/B6**
Na Zderaze **131/E3**
nábřeží Edvarda Beneše **128/A3-C2**
nábřeží kapitána Jaroše **129/D2-E2**

nábřeží Ludvíka Svobody **128/C3-129/D3**
Nábřežní **131/D3**
Nad Bertramkou **130/A4-A5**
Nad Královskou oborou **128/B1**
Nad Petruskou **132/C4**
Nad Santoškou **130/B5**
Nad štolou **128/B1-C2**
Nad Václavkou **130/A5-A6**
Nad Vinným potokem **133/E6**
Nad Výšinkou **130/A3**
Nádražní **130/C4-131/D6**
náměstí Curieových **128/B3**
náměstí Jana Palacha **128/B4**
náměstí Jiřího z Lobkovic **133/E2**
náměstí Kinských **130/C2**
náměstí I.P.Pavlova **132/B3**
náměstí Míru **132/C3**
náměstí Pod Emauzy **131/E4**
náměstí Pod kaštany **127/D1**
náměstí Republiky **128/C4**
náměstí Svatopluka Čecha **133/F4**
náměstí Svobody **126/B1**
náměstí Winstona Churchilla **129/E5**
Náplavní **131/E3**
Náprstkova **128/A5-B5**
Narejdiští **128/B3**
Národní **128/A5-B5**
Národní obrany **126/B1-C2**
Nastruze **128/A6-B6**
Navrátilova **128/C6**
Nebovidská **126/C5**
Nekázanka **128/C4-C5**
Neklanova **131/E5**
Nezamyslova **131/F5-F6**
Nitranská **133/E3**
Norská **133/E4**
Nosticova **126/C5**
Novgorodská **133/E5**
Nový Svět **126/A4**
Nuselská **133/D6-E6**
Nuselský most **132/B5**

O
Obloukova **133/E5-F5**
Odborů **128/B6**
Oldřichova **132/A5-B5**
Olivova **129/D5**
Olšanská **133/F1**
Olšanské náměstí **133/E1**
Olympijská **130/A2-B2**
Ondříčkova **133/D2-F1**
Opatovická **128/B6**
Opletalova **128/C6-129/D4**
Orebitská **129/F4**
Orelská **133/E5-F5**
Orlická **133/E2**
Osadní **129/F1**
Ostrčilovo náměstí **131/F5**
Ostrovní **128/A6-B6**
Ostrovského **130/B5-C4**
Otakarova **133/C5-D5**
Ovenecká **128/C1-C2**
Ovocný trh **128/C4**

P
Palackého **128/C5-C6**
Palackého most **131/D3-D4**
Palackého náměstí **131/E3-E4**
Pankrácké náměstí **132/B6**
Panská **128/C5**

Pařížská **128/B3**
Patočkova **126/A4**
Pavla Švandyze Semečic **130/C3**
Peckova **129/F3-F4**
Pelcova **128/C6**
Pelleova **126/C1-C2**
Perlová **128/B5**
Pernerova **129/F3-F4**
Peroutkova **130/A5**
Perucká **132/C4-C5**
Perunova **133/E3**
Pětidomí **128/A1-B1**
Petra Rezka **132/C6**
Petřínská **130/C2-131/D2**
Petrohradská **133/E5-E6**
Petrská **129/D3**
Petrské náměstí **129/D3**
Pevnostní **126/A3**
Pivovarská **130/C5-131/D5**
Plaská **126/C6**
Platnéřská **128/B4**
Plavecká **131/E4**
Plzeňská **130/A4-C4**
Pobřežní **129/F3-E3**
Pod baštami **126/C2-C3**
Pod Brentovou **130/C6**
Pod Bruskou **127/D3**
Pod hradbami **126/A3-B3**
Pod Karlovem **132/B5**
Pod kaštany **126/C2-127/D1**
Pod Kesnerkou **130/C6**
Pod Nuselskými schody **132/C4**
Pod Slovany **131/E4**
Pod sokolovnou **132/C6**
Pod soutratím **133/F5**
Pod Terebkou **132/C6**
Pod Zvonařkou **132/C4**
Podolské nábřeží **131/E5-E6**
Podolské schody **132/A6**
podpluko vníka Sochova **129/D1**
Podskalská **131/E4**
Pohořelec **126/A4-A5**
Politických vězňů **128/C5-129/D5**
Polská **129/E6-F6**
Přemyslovská **133/E2-F2**
Preslova **130/C3**
Příběnická **129/E4**
Přibyslavská **133/D1**
Příčná **128/C6**
Přímá **130/A6**
Přípotoční **133/F5**
Prokopova **133/E1-F1**
Prokopovo náměstí **133/E1**
Prokopská **126/C5**
Provaznická **128/C5**
Prvníhopluku **129/E3**
Pštrossova **128/B6**
Purkyňova **128/B5-B6**
Puškinovo náměstí **126/C1**
Půtova **129/D3**

R
Radhošťská **133/F2**
Radlická **130/B6-C4**
Radnické schody **126/B4**
Raisova **126/C1**
Rašínovo nábřeží **131/D3-E5**
Rejskova **132/B5-C5**
Resslova **131/E3**
Revoluční **128/C3**
Rohanské nábřeží **129/F2-F3**
Rokycanova **133/E1**
Romaina Rollanda **127/D1**

Rooseveltova **126/B1-C1**
Rošických **130/C2**
Rostislavova **133/D5-D6**
Rostovská **133/E4-E5**
Rubešova **129/D6**
Rumunská **132/B3-C3**
Ruská **133/E4-F5**
Růžová **129/D5**
Rybalkova **133/D4**
Rybna **128/C3-C4**
Rytířská **128/B5-C5**

Ř
Řásnovka **128/C3**
Řehořova **129/E4**
Řetězová **128/B5**
Řezáčovo náměstí **129/D1**
Řeznická **128/B6-C6**
Říčanská **133/F3-F4**
Říční **126/C6**
Římská **132/B2-C3**
Řipska **133/E2-E3**

S
Salmovská **131/F3**
Samcova **129/D3**
Sámova **133/D5-E5**
Sarajevská **132/B5-C5**
Sauerova **133/E1**
Sázavská **132/C3**
Schnirchova **129/D1**
Seifertova **129/E5-F5**
Sekaninova **128/C4-131/D4**
Seminárni **126/A1**
Senovážná **128/C4-131/D4**
Senovážné náměstí **129/D4**
Sevastopolská **133/D4**
Sezimova **132/C5-C6**
Sibiřské náměstí **126/C1**
Skalecká **129/D2**
Skořepka **128/B5**
Sládkova **128/B1**
Sladkovského náměstí **133/E1**
Slavíčkova **127/D2**
Slavíkova **129/F6**
Slavojova **132/A5-A6**
Slezská **132/C3-133/F3**
Slovenská **133/D4-E4**
Slovinská **133/F4**
Slunná **126/A2**
Smetanovo nábřeží **128/A5**
Smolenská **133/E4**
Sněmovní **126/C4**
Sobotecká **133/E3**
Sochařská **128/C1**
Sokolovská **129/E3-F3**
Sokolská **132/B3-B4**
Soukenická **128/C3-129/D3**
Spálená **128/B5-B6**
Sportovní **133/E5**
Spytihněvova **132/B5**
Srbská **126/C2**
Stárkova **129/D3**
Staroměstské náměstí **128/B4**
Staropramenná **130/C4-131/D4**
Strahovská **126/A5**
Strahovský tunel **130/A2**
Strakonická **131/D6**
Stříbrná **128/B5**
Strojnicka **128/C1-129/D1**
Strosmayerovo náměstí **129/D2**
Stroupežnického **130/C4**

Studentská **126/A1**
Studničkova **131/F4-F5**
Stupkova **129/F1**
Sudoměřská **133/F2**
Sukova **126/B1-C1**
Svatoplukova **132/B5**
Svatoslavova **132/C6-133/D6**
Svatovítská **126/B2-B3**
Světlé **128/B5**
Svoboda **131/E5**
Svornosti **131/D4-D5**

Š

Šafaříková **132/B4-C4**
Šeříková **126/C6**
Šermířská **130/B2**
Ševčikova **133/D2**
Šimáčkova **129/D1**
Široká **128/B4**
Školská **128/C6**
Škrétova **129/D6**
Škroupovo náměstí **133/D2-E2**
Šmeralova **128/B1-C1**
Šmilovského **133/D4**
Šolinova **126/A1-B1**
Španělská **129/D6**
Štefánikova **130/C2-C4**
Štefánikův most **128/C2-C3**
Štěpánská **131/F2-F3**
Šternberkova **129/D1**
Štítného **133/E1**
Štorkánova **130/A6**
Štupartská **128/C4**
Šumavská **133/D3-D4**
Švédská **130/A3-B3**

T

Táboritská **133/E1-F1**
Táborská **132/C6-133/D6**
Technicka **126/A1**
Templová **128/C4**
Terronská **126/B1**
Těšnov **129/D3**
Thákurova **126/A1**
Thunovská **126/C4**
Tolstého **133/F4**
Tomášská **126/C4**
Iovarní **129/E1-F1**
Trocnovská **129/E4**
Trojanova **131/D3-E3**
Trojická **131/E4**
Truhlářská **128/C4-129/D3**
Tržiště **126/C5**
Třebízského **133/D2-D3**
Turistická **130/A2-A3**
Tusarova **129/E1-F1**
Tychonova **126/C3**
Tylovo náměstí **132/B3**
Týnská **128/C4**
Tyršova **132/B3-B4**

U

U akademie **128/C1**
U Bruských kasáren **127/D3**
U Bulhara **129/D4**
U garáži **129/E1**
U Havlíčkových sadů **133/D4**
U Kanálky **133/D2-D3**
U kasáren **126/B4**
U křížku **133/D6**
U letenské vodárny **128/B1**

U letenského sadu **128/C2**
U lužického semináře **127/D4-D5**
U Malvazinky **130/A6-B6**
U milosrdných **128/B3-C3**
U Mrázovky **130/A5**
U nádražní lávky **129/F3**
U nemocenské pojišťovny **129/D3**
U nemocnice **131/E3-F3**
U Nesypky **130/A3**
U Nikolajky **130/B5**
U obecního dvora **128/C3**
U památníku **129/F4**
U Písecké brány **126/C3**
U plovárny **127/D3**
U podolského sanatoria **131/E6-F6**
U Prašného mostu **126/B3-B4**
U půjčovny **129/D5**
U Rajské zahrady **129/E5-F5**
U Šalamounky **130/A5**
U Santošky **130/B5**
U seřadiště **133/E6-F5**
U smaltovny **129/D1**
U smíchovského hřbitova **130/A5-A6**
U Sovových mlýnů **127/D5**
U Sparty **128/B1**
U starého hřbitova **128/B3-B4**
U studánky **128/C1**
U topíren **129/E1**
U Trojice **130/B4**
U tržnice **133/D3**
U vodárny **133/E3**
U Vorlíků **127/D2**
U železné lávky **127/D4**
U Zvonařky **132/C4**
Uhelný trh **128/B5**
Újezd **126/C5-C6**
Ukrajinska **133/D5-E5**
Umělecká **128/C1**
Uralská **126/C1**
Uruguayská **132/C3**
Úvoz Nerudova **126/A4-C4**

V

V celnici **129/D4**
V cipu **128/C5**
V Horkách **133/D6-E6**
V jámě **128/C6**
V kotcích **128/B5**
V pevnosti **132/A6**
V tišině **127/D1**
V tůních **131/F3**
V.P.Čkalova **126/B2-C2**
Václavkova **126/B2**
Václavská **131/E3**
Václavské náměstí **128/C5-129/D6**
Valdštejnská **126/C4-127/D4**
Valdštejnské náměstí **126/C4**
Valentinská **128/B4**
Vaníčkova **130/A1-A2**
Varšavská **132/C3-C4**
Vbotanice **130/C3**
Ve Smečkách **128/C6**
Vejvodova **128/B5**
Velehradská **133/E2**
Veletržní **128/C1-129/D1**
Velflíkova **126/A1-B1**
Velkopřevorské náměstí **126/C5**
Verdunská **126/B1-C1**
Veverkova **129/D1-D2**
Vězeňská **128/B4-C3**
Viktora Huga **130/C3**
Vinařického **131/E4-E5**

Viničná **132/A3-A4**
Vinohradská **132/B2-133/F2**
Víta Nejedlého **129/F5**
Vítězná **130/C2**
Vítězné náměstí **126/B1-B2**
Vítkova **129/E3-F4**
Vjirchářích **128/B6**
Vladimírova **133/D6**
Vladislavova **128/B6**
Vlaška **126/B5-C5**
Vlastislavova **133/D5-D6**
Vlkova **129/F5**
Vltavská **130/C4-131/D4**
Vnislavova **131/E5**
Vocelova **132/B3**
Vodičkova **131/E3-F1**
Vodní **130/C2-131/D2**
Vojtěšská **128/B6**
Voroněžská **133/D4**
Voršilská **128/B5-B6**
Votočkova **131/F5**
Vozová **129/E5**
Vratislavova **131/E5**
Vrázova **131/D4**
Vrchlického **130/A4**
Vršovická **133/D5-F5**
Vršovické náměstí **133/E4**
Vršovického nádraží **133/D5**
Všehrdova **126/C5-C6**
Vyšehradská **131/E4-E5**

W

Washingtonova **129/D5-D6**
Wenzigova **132/B4**
Wilsonova **129/D6-E3**
Wolkerova **127/D1**
Wuchterlova **126/C2**

X

Xaveriova **130/A6**

Z

Za Pořičskou bránou **129/E3**
Za viaduktem **129/E1**
Za Ženskými domovy **130/C4-C5**
Záhřebská **132/C3-C4**
Zámecká **126/C4**
Zapova **130/A3**
Závišova **132/C5**
Zborovská **130/C2-131/D4**
Zikova **126/A1**
Zlatá **128/B5**
Zlatnická **129/D3-D4**
Zubatého **130/C3**

Ž

Žatecká **128/B4**
Žateckých **132/B6-C6**
Železná **128/B4-C4**
Žitná **128/B6-C6**
Žitomírská **133/E5-F4**
Žižkovo náměstí **133/E2**

KEY TO STREET ATLAS

Dálnice Motorway		Autobahn Autoroute
Čtyřstopá silnice Road with four lanes		Vierspurige Straße Route à quatre voies
Průjezdní silnice Thoroughfare		Durchgangsstraße Route de transit
Hlavní silnice Main road		Hauptstraße Route principale
Ostatní silnice Other roads		Sonstige Straßen Autres routes
Jednosměrná ulice - Informace One-way street - Information	→ ⓘ	Einbahnstraße - Information Rue à sens unique - Information
Pěší zóna Pedestrian zone		Fußgängerzone Zone piétonne
Hlavní železnice s stanicí Main railway with station		Hauptbahn mit Bahnhof Chemin de fer principal avec gare
Přístaviště Landing place	⚓	Anlegestelle Embarcadère
Metro Underground	· · ӠMʞÆ · ·	U-Bahn Métro
Tramvaj Tramway		Straßenbahn Tramway
Zajímavý kostel - Ostatní kostel Church of interest - Other church	✠ ⊞	Sehenswerte Kirche - Sonstige Kirche Église remarquable - Autre église
Synagoga Synagogue	✡	Synagoge Synagogue
Parkoviště Parking place	ℙ	Parkplatz Parking
Noclehárna mládeže Youth hostel	▲	Jugendherberge Auberge de jeunesse
Pomník - Policie Monument - Police station	⚇ ●	Denkmal - Polizeistation Monument - Poste de police
Věž - Rozhlasová věž Tower - Radio tower	⚲ ⚡	Turm - Funkturm Tour - Tour radio
Nemocnice - Poštovní úřad Hospital - Post office	⊕ ✉	Krankenhaus - Postamt Hôpital - Bureau de poste
Zastavěná plocha, veřejná budova Built-up area, public building		Bebaute Fläche, öffentliches Gebäude Zone bâtie, bâtiment public
Průmyslová plocha Industrial area		Industriegelände Zone industrielle
Park, les Park, forest		Park, Wald Parc, bois
Vinice Vineyard		Weinberg Vignoble
Městské procházky Trips & Tours		Stadtspaziergänge Promenades en ville
MARCO POLO Highlight		MARCO POLO Highlight

INDEX

This index lists all sights, museums and destinations plus the main squares and streets, the key terms and people featured in this guide. Numbers in bold indicate a main entry.

Basilica of St George 30
Beer Museum (Pivovarské Muzeum) 53
Bethlehem Chapel (Betlemské kaple) 46
Botanical Garden 104
Brahe, Tycho 14, 34, 52
Březnov monastery 47
Čapek, Karel 59
Černý, David 101, 105
Čertovka 38
Charles IV. 14, 29, 35, 44, 47, 48, 53, 54, 60, 104
Charles Bridge (Karlův most) 13, 24, 26, 27, 47, 61, 68, 72, 105, 113
Charles Square 104
Charles University (Univerzita Karlova) 48
Children's Island (Dětský ostrov) 106
Church of Our Lady of the Snows (Kostel Panny Marie Sněžné) 54
Collection of Modern Art (Sbírka moderního umění) 61
Comenius Museum (Pedagogické muzeum J. A. Komenského) 38
Convent of St Agnes (Anežský Klášter) 42
Daliborka Tower 31
Dancing House (Tančící dům) 47, 53, 58
Defenestration of Prague 13, 36
Dientzenhofer, Kilian Ignaz 33, 39, 54
DOX 61
Dubček, Alexander 14, 23
Dvořák Museum (Muzeum Antonína Dvořáka) 34, 53, 103
Dvořák, Antonín 50, 53, 59
Einstein, Albert 46
Emmaus Monastery 104
Estates Theatre (Stavovské divadlo) 25, 51, 91
Exhibition Grounds (Výstaviště) 47, 90, 108
Forman, Miloš 23, 29, 33
Franciscan Garden (Františkánská zahrada) 54, 67, 101
Franz Kafka Museum 38
Genscher, Hans-Dietrich 105
Golden Lane (Zlatá ulička) 24, 31
Gott, Karel 21, 52, 78, 90, 100, 113
Guttmann, Robert 78
Hašek, Jaroslav 66, 103
Havel market (Havelský trh) 80
Havel, Václav 11, 29, 39, 53, 58, 66, 79, 91
Holešovice 60, 97, 99
House of the Black Madonna (U Černé matky Boží) 18, 46, 67
Hrabal, Bohumil 83
Hradčany 24, 28, 47, 67, 69, 71, 87, 97, 107
Hunger Wall 104
Hus, Jan 46, 108

Infant Jesus of Prague 39
Jewish Museum 42, 43, 49, 51
Jewish Quarter 25, 41
Ježek Museum (Památník Jaroslava Ježka) 46
Kafka, Franz 11, 22, 31, 32, 46, 52, 62, 66, 76, 112
Kampa 24, 37, 38, 39
Kampa Museum (Muzeum Kampa) 39
Karlštejn 62
Kinsky Summer Palace 104
Kisch, Egon Erwin 11, 32, 66, 100
Klausova Synagogue (Klausova synagoga) 48
Lada, Josef 103
Lapidarium 34, 61
Laterna Magika 55, 56, 91, 102
Lesser Town Bridge Tower 48
Letná 60, 61, 68, 90
Lobkowicz Palais 105
Loreta Shrine (Loreta) 33
Maiselova Synagogue (Maiselova synagoga) 49
Maria Theresia 29
Marksman's Island 34
Mini-Eiffel Tower 104
Mirror Maze (Bludiště) 105, 106, 113, 114
Mozart, Wolfgang Amadeus 26, 39, 51, 61, 102
Mucha Museum 56
Mucha, Alfons 35, 56, 59
Municipal House (Obecní dům) 25, 50, 66, 86, 90, 108
Museum of Communism (Muzeum komunismu) 54
Museum of Decorative Arts (Uměleckoprůmyslové muzeum) 49
Museum of the Resistance (Památník Hrdinů) 56
Music Museum (České muzeum hudby) 39
Na příkopě 74
Národní třída 74
National Gallery (Národní galerie) 34, 104
National Museum (Národní muzeum) 34, 56
National Technology Museum (Národní technické muzeum) 106
National Theatre (Národní divadlo) 47, 57, 67, 91
Neruda, Jan 59
New Jewish Cemetery (Nový Židovský hřbitov) 22, 62, 94
New World (Nový Svět) 30, 34
O2 Arena 48, 89
Old Jewish Cemetery (Starý Židovský Hřbitov) 25, 42
Old Town Bridge Tower (Staroměstská mostecká věž) 44, 48
Old Town Hall (Staroměstská radnice) 44, 45, 112, 115
Old Town Square (Staroměstské náměstí) 25, 26, 34, 45, 69, 88, 94, 114, 144
Old-New Synagogue (Staronová Synagoga) 25, 44

Our Lady of the Snows Church 54, 101
Palace Gardens of Prague Castle (Palácové zahrady) 39
Palach, Jan 60
Pařížská 74
Parler, Peter 35, 44, 47
Petřín 24, 29, 37, 68, 97, 104, 106, 112, 113
Pinkasova Synagogue (Pinkasova synagoga) 25, 49
Planetárium 108
Pohořelec 30, 47
Powder Tower (Prašná brána) 26, 50, 113, 114
Prague market (Pražská tržnice) 80
Prague Spring 14, 23, 53, 108
Prague's Venice 38
Průhonice 63
Rabbi Löw 43, 44
Reinerová, Lenka 33
Rieger Park 61
Royal Gardens (Královská zahrada) 32
Royal Way 24, 26
Rudolf II 29, 34, 41, 52
Rudolfinum 47, 50, 73, 86, 109
Šárka Valley (Divoká Šárka) 62
Seminary Garden (Seminářská zahrada) 40
Slavín 59
Smetana Museum (Muzeum Bedřicha Smetany) 34, 50
Smetana, Bedřich 46, 50, 57, 59, 91
Smíchov 61
Spanish Synagogue (Španělská synagoga) 25, 51
St Martin in the Wall 102
St Mary the Victorious Church (Kostel Panny Marie Vítězné) 39
St Nicholas Church (Chrám sv. Mikuláše) 39, 86, 113
St Peter and Paul Church 59
St Vitus Cathedral 24, 34
State Opera House (Státní opera) 57, 91
Strahov Library (Strahovská Knihovna) 32
Strahov Monastery 24, 29, 32, 47
Stromovka Park 106
Švejk, Josef 79, 103
Television tower (Televizní věž) 61
Terezín 49, 63
Tipsport Arena 48, 90
Toy Museum (Muzeum hraček) 106
Transport Museum (Muzeum Městské Hromadné Dopravy) 107
Týn Church (Matka Boží před Týnem) 45, 51, 52
Velvet Revolution 11, 14, 33
Villa Amerika 54
Villa Bertramka 61
Villa Müller 18
Vinohrady 61, 72, 95, 97

Vítkov 61
Vladislav Hall 36
Vojan Garden 58
Vrtba Garden (Vrtbovská zahrada) 58
Vyšehrad 47, 53, **59**
Wallenstein Garden (Valdštejnská zahrada) 37, 58

Wallenstein Riding Hall (Valdštejnská jízdárna) 41
Waxworks Museum (Muzeum voskových figurín) 52
Wenceslas I 41, 42
Wenceslas IV 44, 47, 48, 101
Wenceslas Square (Václavské

náměstí) 53, **59**, 67, 69, 74, 80, 96, 100, 101, 103, 107, 144
Žižkov 61, **62**, 82, 88, 89, 95
Žofín 34
Zoo (Zoologická zahrada) 107

WRITE TO US

e-mail: info@marcopologuides.co.uk

Did you have a great holiday?
Is there something on your mind?
Whatever it is, let us know!
Whether you want to praise, alert us
to errors or give us a personal tip –
MARCO POLO would be pleased to
hear from you.
We do everything we can to provide
the very latest information for your trip.

Nevertheless, despite all of our authors' thorough research, errors can creep in. MARCO POLO does not accept any liability for this. Please contact us by e-mail or post.

MARCO POLO Travel Publishing Ltd
Pinewood, Chineham Business Park
Crockford Lane, Chineham
Basingstoke, Hampshire RG24 8AL
United Kingdom

PICTURE CREDITS
Cover Photograph: Huber: Simeone (Charles Bridge and the Old Town Bridge Tower)
Photos: A. Buchholz (1 bottom); CHI-CHI: Sitka Šimáňová (16 centre); DuMont Bildarchiv: Kluyver (42), Martini (right flap, 60), Specht (8, 73); G. Hartmann (12, 22, 24 right, 38, 52, 56, 109); R. Freyer (2 centre top, 3 top, 9, 31, 36, 40, 51, 59, 66, 70 l., 74/75, 87, 94, 102, 104/105, 106/107); Huber: Bernhart (3 centre, 82/83), Simeone (1 top), Picture Finder (124/125); J. Gläser (108); © iStockphoto.com: Mlenny (16 bottom); Kavárna Vesmírna: Dominika Duchková (17 top); LA FABRIKA (16 top); Laif/hemis.fr: Giuglio (3 bottom, 92/93); Laif/Hoogte: Holland (80); Laif: Celentano (112 top), Knop (5), Zanettini (108/109); Look: age Fotostock (2 centre bottom, 23, 26/27), NordicPhotos (24 l.), The Travel Library (10/11); mauritius images: Mac Laren (32); C. Norman (98); p. Paterna (15, 20), D. Renckhoff (18/19, 91, 103, 113); Tomás Soucek (17 bottom); T. Stankiewicz (left flap, 2 top, 2 bottom, 4, 6, 7, 54, 62/63, 64/65, 69, 71, 79, 84, 88/89, 107, 112 bottom); Transit-Archiv: Eisler (35), Härtrich (25, 46, 97, 100/101, 106), Hirth (44/45), vario images: imagebroker (49, 70 right), Kiefer (76)

1ST EDITION 2013
Worldwide Distribution: Marco Polo Travel Publishing Ltd, Pinewood, Chineham Business Park, Crockford Lane, Basingstoke, Hampshire RG24 8AL, United Kingdom. Email: sales@marcopolouk.com
© MAIRDUMONT GmbH & Co. KG, Ostfildern
Chief editors: Michaela Lienemann (concept, managing editor), Marion Zorn (concept, text editor)
Author: Antje Buchholz; editor: Wieland Höhne, Cordula Natusch
Programme supervision: Anita Dahlinger, Ann-Katrin Kutzner, Nikolai Michaelis
Picture editors: Gabriele Forst, Wieland Höhne
What's hot: wunder media, Munich;
Cartography road atlas: © MAIRDUMONT, Ostfildern; Cartography pull-out map: © MAIRDUMONT, Ostfildern
Design: milchhof : atelier, Berlin; Front cover, pull-out map cover, page 1: factor product munich
Translated from German by Paul Fletcher, Suffolk; editor of the English edition: Tony Halliday, Oxford
Prepress: BW-Medien GmbH, Leonberg
Phrase book in cooperation with Ernst Klett Sprachen GmbH, Stuttgart, Editorial by Pons Wörterbücher
All rights reserved. No part of this book may be reproduced, stored in a retrieval system or transmitted in any form or by any means (electronic, mechanical, photocopying, recording or otherwise) without prior written permission from the publisher.
Printed in Germany on non-chlorine bleached paper.

DOS & DON'TS 👆

A few things to bear in mind in Prague

DON'T JUST PARK ANYWHERE

Of the many rumours that circulate about crime in Prague, sadly one thing is true: the city is car-thief heaven. That is why you are advised to park your car in a multi-storey car-park or on a CCTV-monitored site. If you must park on the street (and you will have to feed a parking meter), do not leave anything of value visible and leave the glove compartment open.

DON'T FALL FOR TOURIST TRAPS

Prague stages many great cultural events, but it is easy to be lured into overpriced concerts aimed at unsuspecting tourists. Be particularly wary of ticket sellers dressed as Mozart or wearing colourful costumes. They can be very persistent, but are usually selling tickets to concerts comprising a collection of cheesy classics.

DON'T JUST JUMP INTO THE NEXT TAXI

Always be very careful if you see a taxi waiting outside a tourist attraction, e.g. on the Old Town Square and by Wenceslas Square. It is not unlikely that these cars are fitted with 'doctored' taximeters. Do not negotiate a price. You will probably end up paying more. Stick to reputable companies, such as AAA and Citytaxi. If you suspect a fraud, you should ask for a receipt to show the police.

DO LOOK AFTER YOUR VALUABLES AND DON'T BE TOO TRUSTING

Prague is a peaceful city where you can feel safe anywhere night or day. Nevertheless, wherever tourists congregate, there will be pickpockets. Restaurant rip-offs are another annoyance. Every waiter is entitled to a tip, but do look closely at the bill. If it does not seem right, check the figures with the restaurant manager. If you had no complaints about the service you received, then a tip of about 10 percent is normal.

DO NOT CHANGE MONEY ON THE BLACK MARKET

You are still quite likely to encounter shady characters offering to change money, particularly around Wenceslas Square. Do not be tempted! You may discover later on what Polish złoty look like or even find yourself inside a Prague police station. Also, remember that a bureau de change is not the cheapest place to sell your pounds or your dollars. The easiest way to get hold of some Czech koruny is to use one of the many cash machines.

DO TAKE CARE AT PEDESTRIAN CROSSINGS

Do not always assume that you have an automatic right of way on pedestrian crossings. Car drivers do not always stop. And always look to see whether a tram is approaching. They have priority, even on pedestrian crossings.